SACRED SITES

A Traveler's Guide to North America's Most Powerful, Mystical Landmarks

NATASHA PETERSON

Illustrations by
Deborah A. Ristic

CB

CONTEMPORARY
BOOKS

CHICAGO · NEW YORK

Library of Congress Cataloging-in-Publication Data

Peterson, Natasha.
    Sacred sites : a guidebook for the new age traveler / Natasha
Peterson.
       p.   cm.
    Bibliography: p.
    Includes index.
    ISBN 0-8092-4517-5
      1. United States—Description and travel—1981—Guide-books.
2. Sacred space—United States—Guide-books.   3. New Age
movement.   I. Title.
E158.P47   1989
917.3'04927—dc19   88-39977
                                                  CIP

Published by Contemporary Books, Inc.
180 North Michigan Avenue, Chicago, Illinois 60601
Manufactured in the United States of America
International Standard Book Number: 0-8092-4517-5

Published simultaneously in Canada by Beaverbooks, Ltd.
195 Allstate Parkway, Valleywood Business Park
Markham, Ontario L3R 4T8 Canada

Illustrations by Deborah A. Ristic

To my husband, Scott

Contents

ACKNOWLEDGMENTS

Writing *Sacred Sites* was combination treasure hunt and gigantic puzzle. Every clue, bit, and piece was important and valuable, and I am grateful to everyone who helped me put it all together.

Thank you to:

- All those who shared their knowledge and experience including Ari Davis, Daniel Giamario, Howard Hansen, Vicki Fortner, Jorge Arenivar, Ira Kennedy, Diane Arnold, Sandy Whitman, Chuck Cirino, Jim Wills, Peter Rosen, Lyssa Royal, Barbara Scott, and Jim Malloy.
- Deborah Ristic for her time and talent.
- All the archeoastronomers and archaeologists who illuminate the past. In particular thanks to Sal Trento, Jim Maver, John Eddy, Dick Forbis, and E. C. Krupp for their receptivity, help, and referrals.
- The park rangers and staff of the sites listed herein for their gracious help and knowledge. Their contribution was enormous.

- All my friends at the Bodhi Tree Bookstore.
- The editors and staff of Contemporary Books and RGA Publishing, including Stacy Prince, Jack Artenstein, Ranny Draper, Q. Pierce, Janice Gallagher, and, in particular, Helene Chirinian for getting this whole thing started.
- All the photographers whose pictures help this book come alive, and Terry Etherton and Felisha Murray for their referrals.
- Guides and teachers past and present, including Ruth Gerry, Dane Rudhyar, Carol Bell Knight, and Those Who Walked Before for providing the inspiration.
- To my husband, family, and friends for their encouragement and support. Last but not least, thanks to my daughter Miranda for being so patient about making her debut on the earth plane—after I completed this manuscript.

1
THE EARTH IS
A SACRED SITE

Think back to when you first saw a photograph of the Earth. Not a coastline or a continent or someone's backyard, but one of those astonishing images brought home by the *Apollo* astronauts in 1968. For at least a moment, it was impossible not to be awestruck by the Earth's unique and comforting beauty. Swaddled in an oxygen-rich atmosphere laced with swirling clouds, two-thirds covered by sapphire and cobalt waters, our planet in its rounded glory appeared absolutely vibrant. It was very different from the other planets in the solar system and so unlike the barren moon. "This watery blue ball," one of the astronauts said emotionally. It almost looked alive.

Maybe it is.

Today our vision of the Earth is changing and the belief that our planet is merely an inert mass of swirling elements is being challenged. More and more people now believe that the Earth is as alive as you and I.

For a long time, we humans have been taught that we are the only life form on Earth with a soul, a spirit, an unseen force over and beyond our physical selves. The belief in animism—that all things in nature, even rocks, contain life—has been considered ridiculous. Yet this too is being reevaluated.

Scientists have demonstrated beyond a shadow of a doubt that everything around us—rocks, trees, water, and soil as well as the sea life, animal life, and human beings—is pure energy made of electrons, protons, and neutrons. We spring from the same stardust as the Earth and are evolved from her very substance. Just as we are the children of the Earth, so is all nature. We are indisputably connected.

Ancient peoples upheld the sacred unity and partnership of Mother Earth and Father Sky, the perpetual life-givers. They were worshiped in many guises, as the Mother Goddess and Sun God, the Master of Life and the Great Spirit. Earth and Sky have been exalted in practically all cultures across the planet at one time or another as essential to human well-being. They are eternal.

As much of Western culture springs from European thought, it is important to realize that ancient Europeans revered the Earth as Native Americans have. One could always find solace and comfort in nature, and their rituals included sacred circles and the recognition of the four directions. But throughout the Dark Ages, when Europe slid into serfdom, it was taught that nature and her elements were sinister. Trees were no longer sacred, but contained devils and bogeymen. The once-precious full moon now brought out werewolves. This change of attitude kept the serfs submissive and fearful of the lands of the lords. It was also a way to wrench the populace away from their age-old Earth-worshiping practices which were considered undesirable by those in power because it conflicted with the teachings of the Church.

As Father Sky took on a human countenance and Mother Earth, forcibly or not, faded from consciousness, humans exalted themselves as the highest beings on Earth under God. As a species we became highly mental in our development and out of balance with our hearts and better natures, not recognizing how this new path for Western civilization might also be to our detriment.

The belief that we are separate from nature culminated in

the work of the seventeenth-century French philosopher René Descartes of "I think, therefore I am" fame. Descartes wrote that by understanding the forces of nature and using them to our own ends we could "render ourselves the masters and possessors of nature." Plants, animals—all nature—thus became nothing more than a lot of inert matter and mechanical forces devoid of spirit.

This world view has held sway for centuries. Recently, however, the pendulum has begun to swing back.

In the early seventies, NASA scientist James D. Lovelock formulated the Gaia Theory, aptly named after the ancient Greek goddess of the Earth. Lovelock proposed that all natural matter on the Earth, both animate and inanimate, comprised a single autonomous living being. Needless to add, the Gaia Theory has been highly controversial, though it is now gaining force in scientific circles. Lovelock points out that since the dawn of time the Earth has spawned and then rid herself of thousands of different species. Then, in his most compelling warning, he declares that if we continue our destructive actions and push the Earth too far, her reaction will be the same as in the past: she will shift the old environment and form a new one, getting rid of many of the current species (including you know who) in the process.

At long last, we are returning to full consciousness about the living Earth. She is bigger than we are, has a much longer life span, and is smarter too. We may not need to poison or blow ourselves away because the Earth herself could wipe us out first.

The renaissance of interest in the living Earth and her sacred sites is a trail blazed by proponents of the New Age. With a passionate interest in spiritual growth, psychic ability, planetary renewal, and Native American wisdom, these new seekers are bringing back to our culture valuable knowledge. Within this search, sacred sites are no longer dead remnants of the past but highly charged energy centers that can have real meaning for us today.

Visiting a sacred site is a bold way of recovering what we have lost, not only to be seen, but listened to, touched, meditated in, and heartfelt.

Until recently, most of us have been completely unaware on a conscious level of the special energy found at sacred sites, even though we may have felt it intuitively. The feeling that touches us is why some sites have endured despite almost insurmountable odds and why so many people over time have been attracted to them. England's Stonehenge is the most well-known example of this. On its most basic level, Stonehenge is an interesting curiosity because it is a strangely engineered circle of standing and partially fallen rocks. Yet Stonehenge is far more. Something extraordinary occurs there. People visit Stonehenge not only to see it, but to experience its mystical power.

We all have our own favorite places. Often they are close to home, and we go there to find solitude and clear our heads. These places can even be in the middle of the most distracting, high-stress city. A special place is a romantic thing.

On a different and higher level, there are places far from home that we dream about and are obsessed with, sometimes for years. It is not unusual for these places to appear even in our dreams and meditations. In the same way that we are attracted to different people on a soul level, so we are attracted to different "soul places." Certain places on Earth light up for us as surely as certain individuals do.

If we are lucky, and we are finally able to visit our "personal" sacred site, there is sometimes a sense of déjà vu, that indeed we have been to this place before. At last we are able to match the vision of this faraway place that has danced in our mind's eye with the real thing.

Whether constructed by ancient peoples or designed by the Earth herself, sacred sites are places where people reached for the cosmos to expand their world beyond their physical bodies.

Past civilizations often built their temples and ceremonial centers on the Earth's own energy meridians to draw off her natural power. These energy meridians reflect Earth's electric and/or magnetic fields, which is one reason why palpable energy is so often felt at a sacred site.

Early in this century, Englishman Alfred Watkins discovered that many of Britain's ancient landmarks were connected by perfectly straight roads or paths that were constructed in prehistoric times. He dubbed these roads "ley lines." With the advent of air travel it has since been discovered that there are ley lines linking ancient sites all over the world. The enigmatic lines of the Nazca Valley in Peru, for example, can only be deciphered from the air. Ley lines can be seen criss-crossing the landscape from Bolivia to Britain to China. They also appear in North America, mostly in the Southwest.

An energy meridian's capacity to amplify and transform energy, particularly where two such paths interconnect, is one reason that sacred sites may be referred to as power spots or psychic vortexes. Similar to acupuncture lines and chakras (energy centers on the body), ley lines are considered theoretical because they are yet to be measured by conventional scientific methods. Yet this too is turning around.

Some twenty years ago, three Russian scientists published a scientific paper titled "Is the Earth a Large Crystal?" Their theory was that the planet was originally a crystal comprised of twelve pentagonal facets that formed the earthly dodecahedron and that this "matrix of cosmic energy" was natural to the Earth at the time it was formed. Most intriguing, however, is their hypothesis that the crystalline matrix influenced the locations of many ancient civilizations, earth plate movements, and other planetary activities.

Sacred sites embody these and many other mysteries of our planet. They often display powerful evidence of the advanced and sometimes startling capabilities of ancient cultures. These mysteries include lost civilizations, visits by spirit guides and possibly extraterrestrials, earthworks that seem to make sense only from the air, and suspected keys to higher forms of knowledge. Unfortunately, the bright lights of their wisdom still only glimmer for us as most of their messages have yet to be deciphered. Nevertheless, even without knowing the whys and wherefores of a sacred site, the experience of visiting one can be powerful.

These special places speak to us about our spiritual connectedness with all beings over time and the eternal impulse to explore higher forces beyond our bodies. If we open our minds and hearts to receive their message, they can stimulate, heal, and change us.

SACRED SITES OF NORTH AMERICA

Throughout much of this century, the focus for enlightenment has been considered to be India and Tibet. But no longer. The energy is now shifting across the Pacific and focusing on the Western Hemisphere.

North America is a land of tremendous depth. Beyond the homogenous style of our modern lives, with its restaurant chains, shopping malls, and gas station logos, is a land full of ancient history, unique and wild landscape, thrilling beauty, and unexplained phenomena. As it is time to rethink the Earth, so it is time to rethink American land.

The sites included in this book represent a broad spectrum of the type to be found in North America. A few of them are well known. Others are quite obscure. Some are the ruins of ancient American cultures, and others defy explanation altogether. Still others were not built by humans at all, but wrought by nature. More than any other continent, North America possesses a bounty of natural sites.

These power spots exist in silent testimony throughout the modern landscape, from city centers to the isolated wilderness, off interstate highways and just past unmarked dirt roads. Some of the sites have been well preserved, even reconstructed. Still others are tatters of their former glory. What is important is their shared quality of reaching across time and out of it, from the present to the past to the future. They are signposts that serve to remind us we just may not know it all.

Most of them are now part of the national or state park

systems. They range from the most urbanized expanses, complete with sidewalks, manicured gardens, and drinking fountains, to the most primeval forests and desert lands. Many have overnight camping facilities. Those with limited access hours often have campgrounds nearby that will enable you to spend more time close to the site. Although directions are included, keep in mind that new highways get built and old ones get altered.

The book is loosely divided by region—loosely only because I had to compromise between geography and the type of sites represented in each region. For example, the ruins of Cahokia are in southern Illinois, but Cahokia was the religious and social influence for much activity throughout the Southeast. It bridges both regions.

By including some of the history and archaeology of the sites and their former residents, along with a spiritual focus, I am hoping to do some justice to the complex pre-Columbian societies that lived for so long on North American land. Their accomplishments were great. They were far more than "primitive peoples," "cave dwellers," "basket weavers," or any other of the facile labels they have been stuck with. In some ways, they were more advanced than we are today. Also, getting a sense of their lifestyles brings their spirits so much closer to us when we visit the places in which they lived and worshiped.

Even knowing some of the latest scientific discoveries about the sites is knowing only the bare bones. Much of what we know is conjecture—a few known facts and a bit of mythology—we probably know more in our collective unconsciousness. After visiting a sacred site, most of what we are left with is the sheer truth of our own experience.

You may notice that three great power spots of North America—Niagara Falls, Yellowstone National Park, and the Grand Canyon—are not included in this book. Certainly these places have been sources of awe and inspiration to all people past and present. Certainly everyone should see them at least once in their lifetime. But the big three are highly commercialized and well publicized. They are, so to speak, holding their own. One of the goals of *Sacred Sites* is to introduce something new.

Interwoven with the tales of the sites are some personal stories of visits that you can compare to your own experiences. Some reflect a light "let's see" type of attitude. Others involve the Native American-based wilderness experience called a *vision quest.* Vision quest stems from the shamanic tradition that believes it is far better to learn from nature than from people. In these stories, the individual went to a site specifically to do some inner work. The experience can sometimes become quite challenging but often yields profound results.

I don't recommend you do a vision quest unless you are well schooled and have moved gradually onto this level of spiritual work. You wouldn't jump a horse over a six-foot fence without training, would you? Suggestions and tips for enjoying and using a sacred site, as well as the vision quest experience itself, can be found in Chapter 2, "Visiting a Sacred Site."

So whether you are doing some armchair traveling or getting ready for a pilgrimage, welcome to the ancient worlds of North America. They are places that combine science with legend, reality with mystery, and physical beauty with metaphysical experience. Once you have taken the plunge, life on Earth may never feel quite the same again.

2
VISITING A SACRED SITE

When venturing into the wilderness, the home of most of North America's sacred sites, the best advice is also the most basic. As the Boy Scouts say, "Be prepared." They should know. For decades, they have ventured into and diligently cared for American wilderness.

It is often enough to garner the feelings and gifts a sacred site has to offer without the bonus of sunburn, bears that just ate all your food, bitter cold, or getting lost.

North America is vast, with extremely variable topography and climate. One region's dense rainfall is another's threat of dehydration. You can experience sunstroke conditions in the morning in the Colorado Desert and ten hours later have hypothermia on Shasta. Unless you are a veteran camper and backpacker, checking ahead is strongly advised and could save your hide. It is not only unpredictable weather or animals you should learn about; but also the attitude of the local population toward strangers. As one solitude hound told me, "I'm always comfortable in the wilderness. I feel like nature will take care of me. My shackles go up only when I encounter other people. Sometimes I think the only fearsome thing in the forest is man."

Because most of the sites listed here fall under the juris-diction of the national and state park services, a little re-search should be a breeze and is highly recommended. If you are venturing into other areas, the local Land Use and Management Department can tell you all you need to know.

Especially if you are planning to do some inner and spiritual work or psychic venturing at a sacred site, you may want to visit when there is the least chance of running into a herd of school buses filled with singing kids. "One Hundred Bottles of Beer on the Wall" isn't exactly conducive to a meditative state. The same goes for the height of tourist season at some of the more popular sites. Check ahead for quieter hours, off days and seasons. Even though the ma-jority of people visit the Badlands during July and August, for example, the rangers there emphasize the solitude and beauty of the area in spring and autumn.

Park rangers and site personnel are a special breed of human. You can depend on them to be consistently helpful and patient. They are also a tremendous source of informa-tion about the grounds you are visiting. Besides technical information they freely hand out, their general knowledge, stories, and anecdotes about the grounds are fascinating.

Many of the sites also sponsor evening lectures and special tours for those who want to learn more about the archaeology or latest astronomical finds. Some even offer archaeological internships. They often have museum shops that offer a unique collection of books, locally made jew-elry, crafts, and artifact replicas not found anywhere else.

Many of the sites have limited access hours and close at dusk. Nevertheless, it is often possible for groups or individ-uals to get special permission to use the grounds for cere-monies (e.g., sunrise or solstice ceremonies) or medita-tions before or after hours. Most of the groups sponsoring earth celebrations did this without problems. The site's superintendent or manager is usually in charge of this, or a park ranger can refer you to the right person.

Visiting sacred grounds entails some responsibility. It is important to treat the place properly and not leave traces of your visit. (The permanent imprint of your visit is in spirit anyway.) For overnighters, the expression for this is *min-imum-impact camping*. One of the handouts given to visitors who travel to Enchanted Rock, Texas, states it all quite beautifully:

> You are about to enter a primitive hiking and camping area, an experience far removed from the everyday "civilized" life to which we have all become accustomed. The country through which you will walk is being allowed to revert to its natural condition; the incursions of man will be kept to a minimum. The visitor is encouraged to maximize his experience in this natural setting by closely examining and experiencing the sounds, smells and feel of nature. In doing so, the trail in front of you will not only be more enjoyable, but inspirational as well. . . . The satisfaction and achievement of traveling through and camping in a primitive area will be complete only if you, the user, leave no sign of your visit . . . no perceptible traces. Help preserve the harmony and nature of the back country.

Which brings us to a thorny issue: what to do if you encounter vandals, looters, illegal hunting, or toxic waste dumping. In this case, you should follow the example of a very wise little animal called the possum. When faced with danger, the possum pretends it is dead until the coast is clear. So play possum, thereby posing no threat to anyone, including yourself. Smile and leave. When the coast is clear, report the incident to the authorities.

As mentioned above, a visit can and should be inspirational. That is the gift that is yours to receive. If you are interested in visiting a sacred site for the higher experience as much as the look-see, here are some tips and suggestions.

On the metaphysical level, the best advice is a slight but wise elaboration on the scout saying. To paraphrase the samurai warrior credo, "Expect nothing, be prepared for anything."

A visit to a sacred site, like all of life's experiences, may evolve from the energy and mind-set you bring to it. Granted, some sites will grab you more than others. Nevertheless, if you feel angry or are in a negative and resistant frame of mind before going, take a few deep breaths and try to work through it. Otherwise the energy at the site may only serve to amplify what you are feeling. Should you arrive with set expectations, you may end up confused by experiencing something quite different and not realize its value.

Don't go as a tourist. The energy is there. Be perceptive. Find a quiet spot and use whatever stress reduction and meditation techniques you like to help you clear your mind. This will also help you detach yourself from day-to-day activities and concerns. Let go of your cares and worries and let yourself sink into a relaxed frame of mind.

AN ENERGIZING MEDITATION

Here is an excellent step-by-step meditation that will help you reduce stress and tune into the site's energy. Its origin goes back to deep antiquity, derived from the esoteric Mystery School teachings for higher spiritual knowledge. It was used for sensory development.

Each step promotes awareness of the five senses and the four elements—earth, water, fire, and air—which allows your mutual energies to combine and increases the oneness between you and the site.

First of all, just walk around for a while to accustom yourself, ultimately finding an area where you feel comfortable, perhaps where there aren't too many people, and where you can easily take in the whole environment. Then take notice of your breathing. If it is rushed and hyper, try slowing down a bit.

Begin to notice how the land feels beneath your feet. Become aware of it in a simple and appreciative way, almost the same way a child would, with no preconceived notions. Begin to notice its colors, shape, and smell. Nature in a healthy state—the trees, grass and flowers, snow and rocks—has a beautiful scent. At the same time, notice your own physicality, the landscape of your own body: its curves and shape, skeletal structure, and colors. Become aware of the Earth outside of you as well as your own "site," your own body, and the Earthlike nature within, how you are both made of the same substances. Let yourself, with each breath, intermingle with the site. Merge with it enough so you can appreciate the site's qualities in a very physical, earthy way. Sense the hum and vibration of the land, the trees, boulders, even the dust.

Once you've connected on the level of the Earth, move on to sensing any water around you—not only a river, lake, or stream, but also any moisture that may be in the air, in the clouds overhead, or in the surrounding brush or foliage. Imagine tasting it for a minute, cool and wet on your tongue. When you feel fully aware of all the water around you, connect it with your own site, your body, the water that flows through you as blood, the moisture in your mouth and eyes. Again, with each breath, feel a sense of combining the water within and without, combining them until one knows the other, becoming attuned to the water vibration of the sacred site.

Move on to the fire vibration. Sense whatever heat energy is around you, be it the warmth from the sun, the shimmering moon, a campfire, or that rising from the land itself. Fire, heat, light—visualize it inside yourself, all 98.6 degrees of heat flowing through your body, the fire within and the light of your mind. Then fuse the warmth of your body with the warmth of the land, the fire in your stomach with the fire of the sun, and the light in your mind with the light qualities of the sacred site.

Then notice the qualities of the air. Hear the wind, whether it is rustling through the grass and trees or is very still. Compare it to the windy movement of your own breathing, the air that flows in and out of the body with every breath. Know that the air that flows in and through the sacred site is the same air you are breathing.

Now put it all together—smell, taste, sight, and hearing—and simply feel the space you are in. Let its energy tap against your fingertips and brush against your skin. Feel it in your heart. Connect with the heart of the site.

From here you should feel yourself in a state of quiet

receptivity in which any number of perceptions may come and go.

Many people who have had some training in Native American ritual add a few other steps to their sacred site experience that you may want to try: salute the Earth by making an offering to the four directions. Acknowledge the Great Spirit. Ask for spiritual guidance and protection. Pray from the heart, not the mind.

Sometimes people receive spirit energy they feel is negative. Should this be the case for you, simply close yourself off and banish it away with a firm "Leave me alone." If you want, surround yourself with a strong, positive force field. Use any image you like: a crystal wall, a white lighted fence. The negativity will fade away if you feel secure in your own powerful, loving energy.

The site's energy can clear away energy blocks that may be holding you back. You can use it to do some creative visualization, crystal meditations, healing, or prayer. You may ask for an indication or guidance in clearing conflicts or seeking a new path to follow. You may receive imagery from past lives or messages from the spiritual hierarchy. In a lighter vein, you may simply want to experiment with ESP or just allow whatever arises to do so. It is a good idea to bring a journal or tape recorder to keep track of your experiences. If you like to draw, bring a sketch pad. Creative endeavors are often enhanced at sacred sites and are very gratifying.

VISION QUEST

The wilderness has always been used throughout the world for initiation and spiritual growth. In the West it is primarily a Native American tradition called *vision quest*. Some aspects of a vision quest, such as creating a sacred space and acknowledging the four directions, were also practiced in ancient Europe.

Vision quest is a more challenging, deeper wilderness experience. When coupled with sacred lands, a vision quest can be profoundly moving and often marks a turning point in one's life. Vision quest is exactly that—asking for and seeking a vision that will offer answers to inner conflicts and lessons to encourage growth.

Vision quest is based on the belief that nature holds the keys to solving problems and gaining wisdom. It also promotes self-reliance and strength because you are learning for yourself rather than being told what to do by another person. Thus the vision quest becomes a microcosm for facing all the challenges in life, including learning to improve your situation.

There are four basic ingredients to any vision quest:

1. *Severing yourself from your normal routine.* This is most easily done by taking a few days off and getting yourself into a wilderness setting where you can't be disturbed easily.
2. *Creating a sacred space around you.* It is a way of acknowledging that you are there for more than a camping trip. Though many people use different rituals, prayers, or invocations, the basic steps include forming a circle, acknowledging the Earth and/or higher powers of the universe, and marking the four cardinal directions with stones. Some people also acknowledge the sky above and ground below. Create the space and then step into it.
3. *Facing the challenge of "wandering into the labyrinth."* In the tradition, you ask for a vision to help you answer the questions affecting your life: "What is my life's path?" "The next step?" "How can I solve this problem?" Once you are enclosed in the sacred space, everything that happens is a lesson and a synchronistic event. Whatever elicits a response in you is there to teach you, whether it's a trail of ants attacking your campsite, the bitter wind, a shooting star, or the golden sunrise. Your immediate world becomes rich in meaning. It is now your task and responsibility to break through, sacri-

fice the old thought processes that are causing confusion, and go forward.

4. *Reintegrating.* This is the hardest step; wherein you incorporate what you have learned into your daily routine. It is difficult because people often become enchanted with their spiritual experiences but consider them isolated from their day-to-day lives. It should be the opposite. That is why experienced questers say, "A vision not lived never was," or better yet, "You have got to walk your talk." Reintegration is also a valuable way of gaining balance between the spiritual and material worlds.

Native Americans traditionally supported the growth that came from visions. Our society, however, isn't quite as enthused. You have to be judicious as to whom you share your experiences with. It makes the reintegration more difficult, but don't let it prevent you from living what you have learned.

Most people, at least the first few times, do vision quests with a small group of people and a vision quest guide. This is a practical move, especially when venturing into unfamiliar wilderness. As it is, the vision quest process may also be unknown territory, in which case some guidance can be valuable. Vision quest guides cannot and should not take responsibility for your quest but function more in a counseling or buddy system capacity should the going get rough. They know the area and have been on numerous quests. Their knowledge is your guidance. Should a few others also participate on the same quest, each person will have his or her own sacred space. Comparing notes and experiences before returning home can be very rewarding and boost the reintegration process.

Vision quest guides are found through friends and organizations. As for everything else, shop around. It is important that the guide be sensitive to your own level of initiation and wilderness experience.

The vision quest experience can vary greatly. Guide Howard Hansen uses vision quest to challenge himself physically, mentally, and, in the following quest, psychically. As he tells it himself:

"An element of death is important to me on a vision quest. It's not necessary for everyone, but it is for me. I have to feel as though I'm being pushed a little beyond my limits. For some people, just leaving town is enough, but I leave town in pursuit of a strong, powerful experience.

"I went to Shasta with this in mind, and she didn't disappoint me. I left the main campsite and started to climb. Where I was climbing, there had been a few deaths due to the loose shale crumbling underfoot. But I finally mastered a way to do it. I kept going, even though I was hyperventilating and getting tired due to the altitude, which was over thirteen thousand feet. Then I had this vision of a very powerful crystal, so much so that wars had been fought over it. I felt the crystal close by and saw it in the moonlight. A few times I thought I might pass out from exhaustion, but the crystal sustained me and kept me going.

"Somehow I got back to camp alive. I learned then that it was the Night of the Shamans, which is the full moon in Aquarius in late summer. Many of the secret brotherhoods on Shasta have their ceremonies on that night. It is also when the Lemurians (survivors from the lost continent of Mu) expose their most powerful crystal to the moon and recharge their own healing crystals off it. This is what I had seen in my vision. Some geologists say that Shasta wasn't originally part of the continental plate, but moved here and attached itself. It is exactly what people in the Mystery Schools have been saying. It empowers Shasta with a special kind of knowledge, and it empowered me, too."

Howard, along with Daniel Giamario, has taken people on vision quests to power spots in the western U.S. and Hawaii. They related the story of a first vision quest, which was a very different type of experience.

A young woman accompanied them to Joshua Tree to work through some conflicts in her love life. Borrowing a sleeping bag and some other equipment, she excitedly left camp to find a sacred space. Unfocused, she wandered around, got lost, and after searching for the campsite for several hours began to panic and lost the equipment. Around midnight, she wandered back into camp, angry and upset. She was furious at her guides, the desert, and the universe for not giving her the answers she wanted. Despite the guides' counseling, she never did settle down. Finally, weary and unhappy in the predawn hours, it occurred to her that the answer to her quest had been provided: she needed to take responsibility for herself instead of always blaming other people or metaphysical things. Alone, somewhere out in the desert, she had no one but herself to blame for her aimlessness in life, her feeling victimized, not to mention the sleeping bag and equipment she had borrowed and lost. Two days later she left Joshua Tree wiser and not a bit worse for the wear.

Obviously, a vision quest may not always produce a flashy experience. If that is all you are open to, any vision quest guide will tell you not to do it. You have to be open and flexible.

Whether it's an afternoon jaunt, a weekend retreat, or a rough and ready weeklong vision quest, an important part of visiting a sacred site is the direct experience. That's the beauty of it—not simply the mind dance, but feeling it in your heart. It is what makes the visit spiritual.

Sacred sites provide us with the opportunity to stretch beyond the limits of our modern-day thinking to explore and indulge our deepest intuitions about life, love, and spirit. It is a positive search that invigorates and permits us to fit into the eternal puzzle pieces that have for too long been ignored.

Like "be prepared," the final tip for visiting a sacred site is only two words, and they are the most important ones:

Enjoy yourself.

Thunderbird, carry this our prayer
to the sun father that the future
may be bright among us.
Bright and everlasting
as the nourishing waters of the earth mother.
May it be bright above us.
May it be bright below us.
In the daytime may it be bright.
In the nighttime may it be bright.
May the path we follow be filled with plenty
and our numbers increase with our prayers.
Thunderbird carry this prayer to the sun father.
It is finished in beauty.
It is finished in beauty.

Ira Kennedy
Austin, Texas

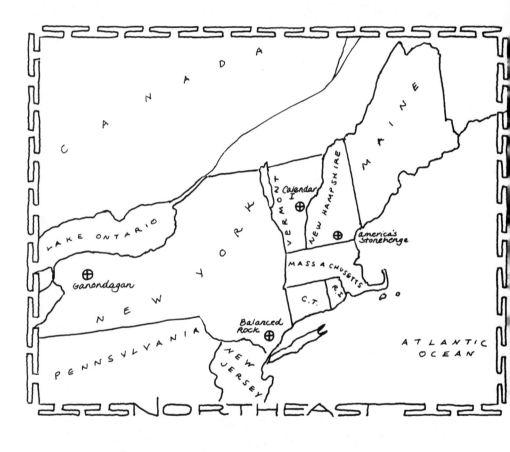

CANADA

LAKE ONTARIO

⊕
Ganondagan

N E W   Y O R K

VERMONT

Calendar
I
⊕

NEW HAMPSHIRE

MAINE

⊕
america's
Stonehenge

M A S S A C H U S E T T S

C.T.

R.I.

P E N N S Y L V A N I A

Balanced
Rock
⊕

N E W
J E R S E Y

ATLANTIC
OCEAN

NORTHEAST

3
THE NORTHEAST: SACRED STONES AND NATIVE AMERICAN DEMOCRACY

All over the Earth there are sacred stones. These megaliths today speak only to the stars. Their full purpose remains hidden and their creators a mystery. Studied, measured, and remeasured by modern people who have sent spaceships to the moon, unraveled DNA, decaffeinated coffee, and ventured ominously into creating life, the stones continue to stand in mocking silence thousands of years after their initial appearance on Earth.

Erected by someone or something, using an unknown system of engineering, the stones appear at first glance to be soulless and inert. But they are not. Through the centuries, long past the demise of their builders, people have gravitated to them as surely as if they were beckoned. As God reigned on his throne in the heavens and the Mother Goddess became a secret in the hearts of those with far memory (intuitive knowledge of ages past), the stones continued to powerfully attract the worship and wrath of the peasantry and ruling classes all over the world.

The new science of archaeoastronomy has heralded a resurgence of interest in standing stones as an attempt is made to unravel their complex mathematical engineering and astronomical alignments with the sun, moon, and stars. Archaeoastronomers have contributed to discrediting the old idea that we today are "advanced" and all those before us were "primitive," with limited brain capacity.

Recently, biologists and geneticists have demonstrated that modern *Homo sapiens* most probably came into being between 90,000 and 180,000 years ago. These early humans, while not educated in the traditional sense, were capable of insight and wisdom. They could think about their place in the universe, and what they concluded does have meaning for us today. The standing stones and their builders can no longer be dismissed. For starters, they tell us of an immense reverence for the sky, intense worship, complex astronomy, and most likely a host of other things we have not yet fathomed.

What could be hundreds of megalithic sites in the United States and Canada have for the most part gone unnoticed. If anything, the discussion of standing stones and sacred circles in America has caused both division and derision in academic circles.

The primary focus of this controversy centers around whether or not there could have been advanced ancient people in America, including European and Mediterranean explorers centuries before Columbus. The consensus of conservative thinkers is that megaliths in America were either left in their precipitous positions by the last ice age or constructed by eighteenth-century colonials.

Fortunately, a handful of dedicated and open-minded researchers are proving otherwise. Through their patient and painstaking work, their discoveries continue to chip away at the stony face of skeptics.

William McGlone and Phillip Leonard, in their book *Ancient Celtic America*, chronicle their investigation of stone epigrams and carvings in America as evidence of ancient Old World peoples in the New World. For example, though the archaic Irish form of writing, Ogham, has been found etched into stones and tablets in Oklahoma, the word in British scientific circles is that Ogham was confined to

Europe. Similarly, though the increasing number of stones found with inscribed Phoenician script in as widely scattered locations as New Hampshire and New Mexico provide evidence that Phoenicians roamed the New World some three thousand years ago, the very idea is pooh-poohed by many who refuse to look beyond what has long been considered fact.

Evidence of ancient voyages made by European, Asian, and African peoples to the Americas long before Columbus has been accumulating for some time. A Hebrew tablet found in Bat Creek, Tennessee, dates back to A.D. 1000. A Viking settlement on the coast of Newfoundland, L'Anse aux Meadows, dates back to about the same time. Chinese scholars claim to have proof that a Buddhist monk named Hui-Shen sailed to Mexico around A.D. 470. A Latin text from the tenth century tells the story of Ireland's St. Brenden, who sailed to a new land in the late sixth century. There are at least ten references to the "land beyond the Pillars of Hercules" (the Rock of Gibraltar) in ancient Mediterranean texts. And then there are all the stories about the Welsh prince Madog ab Owain Gwynedd who in the twelfth century set out with fifty ships and three-hundred crew members and landed in Mobile Bay, resulting in the blue-eyed Mandan Indians of Alabama, whose language included many words found only in old Welsh.

Surely those ancient Europeans that trod American soil would have brought to these shores their tradition of constructing stone sites for worship and marking the sky. However, the acceptance of this theory may not be the problem. It may be in the response of humans to the stones themselves.

By taking a brief look at the history and attitude toward stone settings in Europe, we may be able to understand why they are so unaccounted for on our own shores. As they have done for centuries in Europe, the stones continue to alternately incur passion and disdain in people. Either way, they bring out anything but indifference.

Stonehenge, the product of an unknown civilization's Einstein, is thought to date back to around 3000 B.C. In

Carnac, Brittany, three-thousand standing stones were built with such precision that they may comprise some sort of astronomical computer. These sites predate Pythagorean geometry by two millennia. On Easter Island in the Pacific Ocean, six hundred large stone heads remain an indecipherable puzzle.

When the Druids migrated to Great Britain from central Asia, creating pre-Christian Europe's most prevalent religion, Ireland was the Vatican for their world. It is believed they used the preexisting stone circles for worship and rites, sensitive to the stones' sacred power.

Early Christians, too, were attracted to the stones and used some of them for the foundations of their churches. They may have done this to weaken and hide their pagan power, but it is just as possible that they, too, wished to draw that power into their own religious structures.

As history pushed on, the stones continued to be sites of magical power used for fertility rites, prayers for good crops, and winter solstice celebrations. The young women of Brittany would pour fragrant oils or honey on the stones and slide down them on their bare bottoms to enhance their fertility and goddess powers.

The Christian Church's anger over its failure to crush the allure of the stones, even after the Inquisition and the Reformation, reached an unprecedented height by the eighteenth century. Church leaders in England instituted a policy promoting the whipping, mutilation, and destruction of standing stones and circles. The same century that spawned the U.S. Constitution saw hordes of farmers and other folks roaming the European countryside, ritualistically whipping and gouging the stones.

One farmer so excelled at this activity that he earned the title Stone Killer Robinson. Robinson went so far as to organize teams for the destruction of megalithic sites. What a profession. Dr. William Stukely, a biblical scholar who was also learned in esoteric mystery school teachings, had at the time been studying the stone antiquities and witnessed Stone Killer Robinson and his band at work. Dr. Stukely wrote that it was "as terrible a sight as a Spanish auto-da-fé," a burning or other execution during the Inquisition.

The stones finally became more or less invisible to the general population, though small groups continued to gather at megalithic sites, as did students of metaphysics.

In the twentieth century, the publication of Gerald Hawkins's *Stonehenge Decoded* reopened the doors of interest. Nevertheless, the study of standing stones in the United States has remained an archaeological ugly duckling. But not for much longer. As history shows us, old theories eventually crumble, and megaliths do not.

Because most of the known megalithic structures through the Northeast are scattered about on private land, off the beaten track, or simply stuck in places in the middle of nowhere, overcoming the barriers to visiting them takes some persistence. Sometimes the landowners or local residents are very touchy. Archaeologists who study megalithic sites often share stories like war veterans about getting shot at in the middle of examining a stone setting or inscription. Nevertheless, exploring for megalithic sites in North America is just beginning.

If you would like to visit more stone settings, learn more about megaliths in America, or think you have discovered a stone site, three organizations can provide more information and guidance. Write to the American Institute for Archeological Research, 24 Cross Road, Mt. Vernon, NH 03057, the Middletown Archeological Research Committee (MARC), PO Box 98, Middletown, NY 10940, or the Gungywamp Society, 36 Laurelwood Road, Groton, CT 06340. These organizations can also be helpful if you want information on visiting a site located on private property.

America's Stonehenge at Mystery Hill, New Hampshire

America's Stonehenge at Mystery Hill is a group of stone ruins on twenty acres of private land in North Salem, New Hampshire. Despite its similarities to stone settings in

Europe and other American stone settings, and the dating of some carbon bits found at the site to some thirty-five-hundred years, there is still no commonly accepted conclusion as to its date of origin.

For a long time, this enigmatic stone setting was declared to be the work of farmers living in the area in the eighteenth or nineteenth century, who supposedly built them as storage cellars. The effort and engineering required to place the stones renders this theory impractical. America's Stonehenge continues to defy simple explanations.

Located near the Merrimack River, the site incorporates a stone complex consisting of some twenty-two structures of standing megaliths, dark chambers, granite walls, and stone tunnels. Some of the stones sport ancient inscriptions and were possibly set up for sky alignments.

The deed to the New Hampshire land the site rests on goes back to the early nineteenth century, when it was owned by a farmer named Joseph Pattee. The stone structures were known then as Pattee's Caves. Subsequent half-hearted research into the strange inscriptions proved inconclusive. The Mystery Hill site seemed destined for further obscurity if not total destruction until an enlightened new owner of the land, Robert Stone, opened the site for more study in the early 1960s.

Due to archaeological discoveries connecting this ages-old sacred place to the megalithic sites of Europe, it was renamed America's Stonehenge.

A remarkable feature of America's Stonehenge is its triangular stone monoliths, up to five feet long and three feet wide, which are implanted in the site. Chips and markings on the stones reveal human effort. Upon examination, it is clear that these gargantuan monoliths could not have been left in their present positions by the last ice age. When viewed from a central spot, some of these stones appear to be solar-aligned for solstice and equinox sunrises and sunsets. Recent research supports the calendrical properties of the site, designed in its very construction to harmonize the sky with the Earth. Solstices and equinoxes can

Robert E. Stone

America's Stonehenge—Winter Solstice Monolith

still be observed according to the stones' plan. As astronomy was completely tied into the religion of both ancient Europeans and Native Americans, the site was undoubtedly a place of worship.

Littered through the site are stone slabs up to fifteen feet long that were left lying on the ground, as if their placement or construction had not been completed. Nearby there is evidence of ancient stone quarrying.

Some of the stone inscriptions found at America's Stonehenge have been translated by Barry Fell, author of *Saga America*, as referring to the Phoenician Sun God Baal. Others pay tribute to the Celtic Sun God Bel, essentially the same deity. For both cultures, their Sun Gods reigned supreme. Inscriptions in different languages could also mean that this astronomical observatory and ceremonial center was known and used by travelers from various cultures at different times.

The Sacrificial Table, human in size, is a 4.5-ton granite slab with grooves in it. Supported by additional stones, it rests in front of the Oracle Chamber. A speaking tube of stone connects the table with the chamber. To dub this particular structure a sacrificial altar meant that someone had seen too many horror movies. The granite slab could just as easily have been named the Fertility Table as a tribute to an ancient Earth Goddess.

It should not be assumed that this ancient stone structure was built only for and by Europeans. Native Americans may have been involved. If Europeans were there at sometime in the misty past, there must have been some trading and intermarriage between them and the local residents.

America's Stonehenge is just the beginning of bringing to light the momentous beauty and power of the standing stones of ancient America.

Robert E. Stone

America's Stonehenge—The Sacrificial Table

America's Stonehenge at Mystery Hill is found outside North Salem, New Hampshire. Take Route 111 east off Interstate 93 (Exit 3), then take a right on Island Pond Road and a right onto the marked entrance. The site is open weekends in April and November, then seven days a week May through October, closing at dusk. It is possible for groups or individuals to obtain permission to be present for solstice or equinox risings and services. For more information, write to or call America's Stonehenge, PO Box 84, North Salem, NH 03073; (603) 893-8300.

Balanced Rock, New York

Megaliths are classified as two basic types: dolmens and menhirs. A dolmen features a huge stone balanced on several smaller stone supports. A menhir is a standing stone, whether isolated or in a group. The Sacrificial Table at America's Stonehenge (see preceding site) is a dolmen. Some dolmens were used as burial crypts for honored individuals of the community. One or more bodies were placed underneath the resting stone with their burial objects, and the entire structure was covered with earth.

Dolmens can be found all over Great Britain, and there is a magnificent dolmen off the main road in the small town of North Salem, New York.

Called Balanced Rock, it is a stunning 2,240-cubic-foot boulder of solid pink granite weighing some ninety tons. Balanced Rock is exquisitely positioned on several cone-shaped limestone supports. A decade ago, archaeologist Salvatore Michael Trento and his team of researchers took aerial shots of Balanced Rock and the surrounding grounds. They discovered three circular earthen rings that were revealed by discolorations in the soil. Balanced Rock may have been part of a larger ancient stone complex that begs for further investigation.

Balanced Rock is located on Route 116 near Keeler Lane in North Salem, New York. It is about 10 yards off the highway near the town's main post office.

Calendar One, Vermont

Inside a circular ring of earthen ridges at Vermont's quiet Calendar One site, a natural spring carries crystal-fresh water to the surface. Fifty yards away are an earthen mound and a stone chamber. To the east, nearby, are two standing stones. To the west is a stone wall made of granite boulders. On two of the large stones placed alongside the north-south wall, some carved crosshatchlike inscriptions similar to others found in Europe associated with sun worship can be found. In the corners of the stone chambers, polished stones have been discovered.

The investigation of Calendar One is a good example of the work dedicated amateurs can do. Amateur archaeologists Byron Dix and James Mavor studied Calendar One in the late 70s for its possible sky alignments. The results of their research were not only numbers, astronomical alignments, azimuths, and the like, but as well the strong feelings that Calendar One most certainly was a sacred place for many years. Sacredness, however, can only be felt, not measured.

Dix discovered that at a specific observation point inside the earthen ring, a calendar including the natural and built features of the spot comes into play. The eight most sacred and important solar events—summer and winter solstice sunrises and sunsets and spring and autumn equinox sunrises and sunsets—are marked, an indication that the site could be the remains of another ancient computer. Dix and Mavor's study of Calendar One includes almost two dozen alignments with the sun, moon, and stars. What a special place to spend some time in.

Calendar One is on private land about 20 miles north of South Woodstock, Vermont. Like most sites on private land, it is not open to the general public. By writing one of the two archaeological organizations listed in the introduction to this chapter, you may be able to accompany the next archaeological expedition to Calendar One or arrange for a guided visit.

Ganondagan, New York

Ganondagan is a lovely site that includes a large, open grassy plain and a hilly forest filled with maple, oak, hickory, and pine trees. Serene and beautiful to the eye, Ganondagan nevertheless tingles with energy, touching all who visit with its powerful vibration. Five miles of trails are punctuated by markers that tell us the dramatic history of a land that was once a seventeenth century Seneca Indian village and the home of a visionary Native American woman whose insight helped to change the history of the West.

Ganondagan is a site sacred to the Haudenosaunee, or Iroquois, people. It was a town once inhabited by a woman whose role was central in the formation of the great League of Five (later Six) Nations. Her name was Jikonsaseh, but she is also known as the Mother of Nations or the Peace Queen.

The league was founded centuries before Columbus in upstate New York by a prophet named Deganawidah. His name is rarely uttered by the Iroquois, who prefer to refer to him as the Peacemaker. For that is what he was. This brilliant thinker came of age during a time of savage blood feuds and cannibalism. Warfare and revenge were endemic among the northeastern Woodland nations. An introspective young man who is said to have stuttered, Deganawidah developed a philosophy that came to be known as the Great Law of Peace. With his disciple, Hiawatha, the Peacemaker forged five warring tribes—the Mohawk, Onondaga, Seneca, Oneida, and Cayuga—into a federal union of states that came to be known as the great League of Five Nations.

Jikonsaseh is said to have descended directly from the first woman on earth, Sky Woman. She was among the very first to accept Deganawidah's message, but even before pledging herself to the Great Law of Peace she was an important person among the Seneca. She reportedly had a cabin near the trail that was used as a way station by warriors as they traveled to and from battle. Jikonsaseh offered the warriors food and relished the stories they would tell her of battle. "In effect," says Pete Jemison, site director of Ganondagan, "she was just as much a part of the evil that was happening as the ones who were carrying it out, because she fed on the stories."

After hearing the Peacemaker's message, Jikonsaseh recognized the evil in herself and became his disciple. Here is how Jemison, himself a Seneca, relates what happened next:

"The Peacemaker gave her the name Mother of Nations and explained to her that women would have an important role in this peace. He told her that in peace they would be one big family living in a large longhouse with the sky as the ceiling and the earth as the floor. He said that each nation would have fires burning and each nation would have sachems [chiefs with wisdom and responsibilities]. He said the women would have the responsibilities of raising up the chiefs who would come from a matrilineal descent. He said the women would have the responsibility of holding the titles of the chiefs and would be able to remove a chief if he went astray."

Ganondagan was described in 1687 by Frenchman M. L'Abbé De Belmont as being "a city or village of bark, situated at the top of a mountain of earth, to which one rises by three terraces. It appeared to us, from a distance, to be crowned with round towers." In the same year, Ganondagan, Town of Peace, was destroyed by a large French army led by the governor of Canada.

Although the town of Ganondagan, the Peacemaker, and the Mother of Nations all passed from the scene, the mighty League of Five Nations lived on for centuries. Deganawidah has been buried by history, but his ideas, incorporated into the league, held great sway among our founding fathers.

Benjamin Franklin, in particular, was fascinated by the league's federal union of state governments. Each of the Iroquois states conducted its own internal affairs. But when it came to matters of peace or war, or other deliberations that affected the common welfare, the problems would be

debated on the "federal" level before the council of the
league. Other Iroquois principles that had no equal in
European governments of the time included the ideas of
leaders as servants of the people, popular participation in
government, female suffrage, impeachment of officials,
and the importance of public opinion.

Ganondagan is more than Jikonsaseh's hometown. As a
symbol of the great League of the Haudenosaunee, whose
principles were borrowed and interwoven into our own
constitution, it is also a cradle of our own American
democracy.

The Iroquois Nation still exits. Haudenosaunee women
still have great responsibility and power among their people, and their role can be traced back to Jikonsaseh's
liberation at the feet the Peacemaker.

Ganondagan State Historic Site (formerly known as
Gannogaro State Historic Site) is located in the western
Finger Lakes region, 12 miles southeast of Rochester. To
drive there, take Exit 44 off the New York State Thruway
(Interstate 90). Travel Route 332 south to the second traffic
light, then turn right on County Road 41, which becomes
Boughton Hill Road. At the top of the hill, cross the intersec-
tion and park in the second driveway on the right. Located
within Ganondagan are several marked trails, an exhibit
depicting the eight clans of the Seneca and research archives. The site sponsors programs and celebrations during the summer, including an annual Seneca gathering in
mid-July. The trails are open year-round, 8:00 A.M. to
sunset, weather permitting. The visitor center is open from
May through October, Monday to Saturday. Hours vary.
Admission is free. For more information, write to or call
Ganondagan State Historic Site, 1488 Victor-Holcomb Rd.,
Victor, NY 14564; (716) 924-5848.

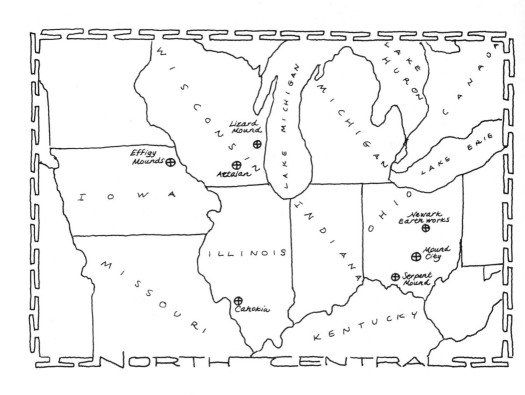

4
THE NORTHCENTRAL: THE MYSTERIOUS MOUND BUILDERS

Great earthen pyramids, burial mounds, and effigies mark the remains of ancient North American civilizations that lasted over twenty-five centuries. Over that period, the Mound Builders included three separate cultures—the Adena, Hopewell, and Mississippians. Geographically, the Adena and Hopewell were centered in the Ohio River basin, and the later Mississippians lived along the great river and throughout the Southeast. Their settlements ranged from Iowa to Florida.

The hallmark of the people of these civilizations was the earthwork, which served a number of purposes. These great achievements of engineering entombed exalted dead, raised on high their religious temples, and ceremonially bridged the gap between the sacred Earth and sky.

The Mound Builders are wholly mysterious, as much as the Anasazi culture of the Southwest. Though many archaeologists conclude the mounds were probably built for worship and death ceremonies, very little is known about the origins and demise of the people that built them.

The Mound Builders appeared around three thousand years ago from places unknown, and the last of them disappeared early in the 1500s. Using rhetoric that echoes theories concerning the demise of the Mayans, scientists theorize the end of the Mound Builders may have come about due to disease or social unrest. The Native American tribes that subsequently lived in areas around the abandoned mound cities also knew little or nothing about their forebears. Only the Chocktaw of what is now the state of Mississippi speak of them in their oral history. They tell the tale of their ancestors from the Southern Empire, who had a vision of their new home across the waters. Fleeing invaders, they sailed north until they hit land and continued up the great river. Could these ancestors have been Mayans, fleeing the Toltec invaders? Like so much about the Mound Builders, it is impossible to know for sure.

The general lack of knowledge on the part of eastern and northeastern tribes helped to fuel outrageous legends and fantastic myths about mysterious lost races, even though the reality of the Mound Builders is as bewildering as the most imaginative fiction.

The Mound Builders and their lavish artifacts first attracted the attention of white settlers early in the eighteenth century. Because the Native Americans of the Midwest were primarily nomadic tribes and labeled "primitive" by the colonists, it was reasoned that the mounds could not have been built by their ancestors. Surely they must be the product of a lost race. For the next one hundred years, this notion was considered an indisputable fact.

The creators of these myths were not mystics or writers of fiction, but rather notable scholars and mainstream scientists. Robert Silverberg, in his fascinating and thorough work, *Mound Builders of Ancient America*, traces the myths and lost race legends of the day. In the late eighteenth century, for example, Ezra Stiles, then president of Yale University, hypothesized that the Mound Builders were of biblical origin, Canaanites who either crossed Asia into America or were transported here by Phoenicians and that they founded the Mayan and Incan civilizations.

Benjamin Franklin, for all his genius, was no closer to the truth. He declared that it was more likely the mounds had been built by the Spanish explorer de Soto. A similar theory espoused was that the mound cities were built by Danish Vikings on their way to founding the Toltec civilization in Mexico. Relating to this was a reputed Indian legend about an ancient albino race in Tennessee that could see only at night and avoided the sun. The legend implied that they were the builders of the mounds.

Thomas Jefferson, a true renaissance man and brilliant thinker, was one of the first to scientifically excavate a mound. "It is too early to form theories on those antiquities," he wrote. "We must wait with patience till more facts are collected."

Words of reason, yet few heeded them. People just would not believe that the earthworks were built by Native Americans. Probably the most popular theory was that the Mound Builders were descendants of the ten lost tribes of Israel. William Penn of Pennsylvania believed that, and so did Oliver Cromwell of England. Others speculated that they were Tartars, Egyptians, Greeks, Phoenicians, or Welsh.

In 1833, a best-selling book of the day declared that America was where Noah's Ark landed and that the Mound Builders were antediluvian. This tied in with Ignatius Donnelly's *Atlantis, the Antediluvian World*, published almost fifty years later, in which he claimed that the Mound Builders were offshoots of the Atlantean colonies of Mexico. The speculation was reaching a fever pitch. The Mound Builders became a favorite subject of romantic novels and poetry. Such works had titles like *The Genius of Oblivion*, "Thanatopsis" by William Cullen Bryant, *Behemoth: A Legend of the Mound Builders*, and *Centeola, the Maid of the Mounds*.

Some of this speculative fiction may have even played a role in the creation of the Mormon Church. Critics of Mormon founder Joseph Smith claimed he was an imaginative boy who was simply carried away by the fiction of the Mound Builders that was so much in vogue during his youth. Two books in particular were mentioned, *Views of the Hebrews—The Tribes of Israel in America* by Reverend Ethan Smith (no relation to Joseph Smith) and *Manuscript*

Found by Reverend Solomon Spaulding. Joseph Smith was charged with having pirated *Manuscript Found*, though no proof of this ever surfaced.

Nevertheless, the critics claimed, there were enough similarities in both books to the Book of Mormon to support their claims. Furthermore, the farm in Vermont where Joseph Smith spent his boyhood is near some of the enigmatic standing stone structures of New England. Whatever the truth may be, the young man may have had brushes with the theories, mysteries, and lore of ancient America long before the vision that founded his new religion.

In 1858, a trader by the name of William Pidgeon published a wild book called *Traditions of De-coo-dah*. Buttressed by his "close friendship" with De-coo-dah, an old Indian mystic who claimed to be the last member of the Elk Nation supposedly descended from the Mound Builders, and drawing upon nearly every legend current at the time, Pidgeon told of the presence in the New World of almost every Old World civilization and their mound-building activities.

Pidgeon interpreted the meaning of some four-hundred earthworks. He told of ancient battles, assassinations, and wars among an original 96 rulers; migration of lost tribes and priesthoods; and their ultimate destruction. The Smithsonian Institution was horrified by *Traditions of De-coo-dah*. But the public's reaction was delight.

Still, the idea that the Mound Builders and Native Americans were somehow related kept resurfacing. As early as 1803, Bishop Madison used Cherokee lore to prove the Mound Builders were really Native American ancestors. This theory was rejected at the time as patently absurd.

Then, quite typical of the racist scientific and religious liturgy being spouted in the nineteenth century, J. W. Foster, president of the Chicago Academy of Sciences, dealt the Indians a particularly vicious blow. He declared the skull formation of Native Americans to be profoundly primitive, using this to degrade their abilities and separate them from the mound-building civilization.

As Silverberg points out, "Here, cloaked in scientific trappings, are the sentiments of a nation then engaged in genocide. . . . The dream of a lost prehistoric race in America was profoundly satisfying. . . . Conscience might ache a bit over the uprooting of the Indians, far from being long-established settlers in the land, were themselves mere intruders who had wantonly shattered the glorious Mound Civilization of old."

Nevertheless, we can state today with much certainty that the Mound Builders were indeed Native Americans.

Most theorists believe that human beings migrated across the Bering Strait from Asia into the New World about twenty thousand years ago, although some evidence points to an even earlier time twice as far back. In 1927, when a crafted stone point was found lodged between the ribs of a bison extinct for ten thousand years, it confirmed that humans were hunting giant sloths, woolly mammoths, mastodons, and saber-toothed tigers in the Americas during the last ice age. But the men and women who came here apparently were not Neanderthal, Cro-Magnon, or anything else. Judging from skeletons of both women and men found in the Adena culture tombs, which were frequently over six feet tall, they were as we are today.

These early Native Americans appear to be mostly big-game-hunting nomadic tribes until about 8000 B.C., when the climate of North America radically changed, becoming warmer and drier. The glaciers withdrew to the north. For the next seven thousand years, hunting and gathering was the predominant lifestyle, with the people grouped in small villages. Then came the agricultural revolution, with the evolution of farming cultures with larger populations and a more structured social order.

The next 1,700 years, from 1000 B.C. to A.D. 700, is referred to as the Burial Mound Period by archaeologists. This is the era of the Adena culture, whose people populated much of Ohio and eastern Indiana and spread into Kentucky, western Pennsylvania, and West Virginia.

Though other mounds had been plundered and ruined

by a greedy nineteenth-century artifact rush, no conclusions were drawn at the time about their builders. The Adena were recognized as a separate culture only in the early part of this century, when scientists excavated a great burial mound on the Adena Estate near Chillicothe, Ohio.

Intriguingly enough, one of the most important artifacts uncovered in the Adena Estate excavation was the Adena pipe. The bowl of this stunning red and yellow clay pipe is in the shape of a man who has a strikingly Mayan face and wears the ear spools signifying a personage of very high rank.

Today we know that the Adena were the first earthwork builders in the Ohio and Mississippi valley regions. Though their exact roots remain unknown, a southern origin, probably the Yucatan, is suspected. It is theorized that the ancestors of the Adena migrated north, rather than being descendants of those who had lived in the area for several centuries. This idea is supported by the fact that some of the skeletons recovered in their burial mounds have skulls that had been deliberately elongated in infancy to be more pointed, a feature of classic Mayan beauty.

The Adena culture was eventually supplanted by another mound-building group, the Hopewell, which lasted into the first millennium A.D. Also named after the estate where they were first differentiated, the Hopewell culture built burial mounds that were much more lavish than those of their predecessors and that differ in important architectural and artistic details. They also apparently did not engage in infant skull manipulation.

Because the majority of weapons, jewelry, pottery, and other artifacts were discovered inside the burial mounds, both societies have been labeled by many archaeologists as being death cults. This is an unfair conclusion, for the Adena and Hopewell had a lot more going for them than fancy graves.Their cultures boasted sophisticated astronomy, agriculture, arts and crafts, social organizations, and forms of worship. Their trade routes extended to the Southwest and the Gulf of Mexico. They made beautiful jewelry and lavish clothing of fine furs and fabric to indulge their own vanity and please their gods and goddesses. They were hunters, farmers, warriors, and artists headed by a class of rulers and priests. The royal bloodlines were matrilineal, and women chose their consorts. Though the population was divided into classes, there is no concrete evidence of social upheaval or wars from within.

Over the ages, in civilizations throughout the world, it is not uncommon for prominent citizens to be buried with their treasures. As both cultures began to disband and die out, it is possible that they buried with their dead what they could not take with them. And other than in honored burial sites and sacred temple grounds, where else would you expect to find community treasures? In the fields? Dumped by the roadsides? In the cooking areas?

Judging from their ruins and artifacts, the Mound Builders were prolific traders and inspired artisans. Items found in the burial mounds include hauntingly beautiful carved pipes, animal and humanlike figurines, and pottery. A large amount of jewelry has also been recovered, fabricated from a variety of materials, including turquoise, mica, copper, marble, shells, flint, polished wood, stone, obsidian from the Southwest, quartz crystal from Appalachia, and shark's teeth from the Gulf of Mexico. Hundreds of thousands of freshwater pearls have also been found.

The wealth of the burial mounds makes perfect sense. Knowing so very little about their lives, their ceremonies, their songs and poetry, and most of all the manner in which they worshiped, it is also easy to understand why with little more than their graves to judge them by, we would think of them as living only for an afterlife. After all, the central image of Christianity is a man nailed to a cross. Would this mean that in a similar situation in a distant time, future archaeologists or extraterrestrial visitors would assume Christianity to be just a cult of pain? Of course it is much more than that. Likewise, the Adena and Hopewell were certainly more than mere death cults. The lives and religion of the Mound Builders deserve a reevaluation.

Besides their burial mounds, the Adena and Hopewell also constructed magnificent earthworks. Some are geo-

metric shapes, and others, known as *effigy mounds*, are in
the form of snakes and other animals of the forest. Some
are huge, others are small. Still others stand in clusters.
Effigy mound building became very important in the latter
Hopewellian era, around A.D. 500. Hundreds of these peculiar constructs have been found in southeastern Wisconsin,
northern Illinois and Indiana, and as far west as Iowa.
(Another, at Mt. Gilead, North Carolina, is included in Chapter 5, which covers the Southeast.) The earthworks are an
enigma. As with all of the effigy earthworks that dot the
planet, the question remains: For whose eyes were they
built when they can be deciphered only from the air?

The Ohio River basin is a hotbed of these ancient American Adena and Hopewell ruins. Though I have covered a
number of them in this chapter, for more information, write
to or call the Ohio Historical Society, 1985 Velma Ave.,
Columbus, OH 43211; (614) 297-2300. Or call the Ohio
Tourism Office toll-free, 1-800-BUCKEYE.

The Serpent Mound State Memorial, Ohio

*After I visited the mound, I often used to
dream of flying with the serpent.*
—Marilyn Bridges, *photographer for* Markings: Aerial
Views of Sacred Landscapes.

The Great Serpent Mound in Ohio is a stunning effigy
earthwork of an uncoiling snake about to swallow a large
oval egg. Artistically, it is perfect—a lively and beautiful
creature with soft, twisting curves. Historically, it is attrib-
uted to the Adena people, though both Adena and Hopewell artifacts were excavated in a nearby conical mound.
Most likely, both cultures used the Great Serpent Mound for
worship during different centuries. Having been built sometime between 1000 B.C. and A.D. 700, it is at least fifteen
hundred years old, possibly three thousand years old.
Stretching across the Ohio landscape, it measures 1,348

feet in length, or approximately one-quarter mile. Twenty feet wide, it rises to a height of between four and five feet. Its open jaw gapes across seventeen feet. The serpent's builders were meticulous in their planning and construction of the mound. According to modern analysis, we know that it originally was outlined on the ground in clay and built up from the outline with earth. Unlike most of the effigy mounds, the Great Serpent was not a burial crypt. No skeletons have ever been found inside.

In 1883, Frederic W. Putnam of the Peabody Museum of American Archaeology and Ethnology at Harvard visited the serpent and later wrote of his visit:

> Leaving the wagon, we scrambled up the steep hillside, and pushing on through the bush and brier were soon following the folds of the great serpent along the hilltop. The most singular sensation of awe and admiration over-whelmed me at this sudden realization of my long cherished admiration, for here before me was the mysterious work of an unknown people and their seemingly most sacred place. Was this a symbol of the old serpent faith, here on the Western continent, which from the earliest time in the religions of the East held so many people enthralled, and formed so important a factor in the development of succeeding religions? Reclining on one of the huge folds of this gigantic serpent, as the last rays of the sun, glancing from distant hilltops, cast their long shadows over the valley, I mused on the probabilities of the past; and there seemed to come to me a picture as of a distant time, and with it came a demand for an interpretation of this mystery. The unknown must become known.

Three years later, when Putnam learned that the serpent was to be leveled to make way for a cornfield, he heroically launched a campaign in Boston to save it. By comparing its destruction to nothing less than destroying Bunker Hill, he raised enough money to buy the land.

Serpents are powerful symbols and primal to all of us. They appear in most of the world's creation myths, some-

Marilyn Bridges

Serpent Mound, Ohio

times as sea serpents or other sea creatures such as dolphins or whales. From culture to culture, serpents alternately represent good and evil knowledge. The plumed serpent looms large in both the Mayan and Aztec cultures as a bringer of wisdom. In Hinduism, the coiled power of the serpent represents enlightenment and creativity. The ancient Celts also built serpentine structures. However, in the West, everyone is familiar with the story of the Garden of Eden, where the serpent—here representing forbidden knowledge—is a symbol of evil.

Because of this universal symbolism, the Great Serpent Mound is considered to have been a very sacred place to its ancient builders and worshipers.

Recently, however, another theory about the origin and meaning of the serpent was offered by psychologist Thaddeus Cowen of Kansas State University. After a thorough study, Cowen proposed that many of the mounds are representations of star groups and constellations. His theory that

The Great Serpent Mound could represent the Little Dipper. Polaris is surrounded by the mystic spiral.

the Great Serpent Mound in effect represents Ursa Minor, or the Little Dipper, is very intriguing, particularly when the serpent mound and the Little Dipper are diagramed side by side. Whatever the connection, the Great Serpent Mound is clearly connected to the sky. Perhaps someday we will know how.

The Serpent Mound State Memorial is in Locust Grove off Route 73 and is maintained by the Ohio Historical Society in Columbus. It is open weekends only in April and May, seven days a week from Memorial Day to Labor Day, weekends until October 31, and then closed through the winter. There is an observation tower on the grounds, so you don't have to rent a plane to get a broad view. You may want to call ahead to get a quiet visiting time, because the serpent is a favorite field trip for school children. Check ahead for days and hours which vary throughout the year. Groups can receive special permission to use the grounds during off hours. For hours and more information, write or call Serpent Mound State Memorial, 3850 State Route 73, Peebles, Ohio 45660; (513) 587-2796.

Another serpent mound exists farther north in Ontario. **Serpent Mounds Provincial Park** in Canada features a serpentine mound and several burial mounds. It is a beautiful park with campgrounds overlooking Rice Lake. For more information, write to or call Serpent Mounds Provincial Park, RR 3, Keene, ON K0L 2G0, Canada; (705) 295-6879.

The Newark, Ohio, Earthworks

Like its namesake in New Jersey, Newark, Ohio is a busy industrial center. At one time, maybe ten centuries ago, four square miles of awesome burial mounds, animal effigies, and geometric earthworks stood there.

The Newark Earthworks once consisted of a large octagon and circle, both some twelve hundred feet in diameter. These two earthworks were connected to two others, a large square and another circle, via long earthen causeways. Two of the original geometric designs, the octagon and adjacent circle that encloses an eagle effigy, survived urban development and are now protected by the state park system.

The meaning and use of geometrically-shaped mounds are much more difficult to speculate upon than animal effigies or burial mounds. It would seem that the site somehow reflected the sky, as the Serpent Mound reflects the Little Dipper, or some sort of map or mathematical formula. In the last few years archaeoastronomers have begun to study the Newark mounds for their possible relationship to heavenly counterparts. We may learn more about these amazing designs in the future.

In order to see all of the Newark Earthworks, it is necessary to travel through a couple of miles of city blocks. Yet despite the urban surroundings, the parks are large enough to retain a semblance of peacefulness and splendor. The three sections comprising the Newark Earthworks are:

Octagon Earthworks. An ages-old octagon is joined by parallel earthen walls to a circle that encloses twenty acres. Inside the octagon are more mounds. The entire setting encompasses 138 acres. It is open daylight hours year round and is surrounded by a golf course.

Mound Builders State Memorial. Incorporating a large circle with earthen walls up to fourteen feet high, the memorial encloses twenty-six acres. It is open Wednesday–Saturday 9:30 A.M. to 5:00 P.M. and 12:00 P.M. to 5:00 P.M. Sundays year round.

Wright Earthworks. Located about a quarter of a mile northeast from the Octagon Earthworks it is part of the original remaining square. It is open daylight hours year round.

To see the **Newark Earthworks**, start at Mound Builders State Memorial, located on the southwestern edge of Newark, Ohio. Take Route 79. When it becomes a two-lane highway, you are at the mound site and museum. The Ohio Indian Art Museum also is situated here and contains numerous Hopewellian artifacts. Museum staff can also provide directions to the other nearby earthworks. After your mind is filled with the images of Hopewell treasures, you can always unpack your golf clubs and draw off the power of the grounds to lower your par. For more information, write to or call Mound Builders State Memorial, 99 Cooper Avenue, Newark, OH 43055; (614) 344-1920.

Mound City Group National Monument, Ohio

The Mound City Group is one of the best-preserved Hopewellian sites. On a peaceful self-guided tour, you can see and experience twenty-three prehistoric mounds that lie on a thirteen-acre tract of land within a low earthen embankment. The mounds have yielded some extraordinary artifacts, including a shaman's "death mask," so labeled arbitrarily by the archaeologist who excavated it, and fragments of mammoth and mastodon tusks. The mounds have been excavated three times, first in 1846, the fruits of which went to the British Museum, then right after World War I, and again in the mid-sixties.

This restored cemetery for the honored dead dates back to 200 B.C. It was called Mound City because there were so many mounds in such a small area that it looked like a town. The nickname is Mound City Necropolis, meaning City of the Dead. Marked trails, an observation deck, and a visitor center are also at the site.

To visit the Mound City Group National Monument, drive about 3 miles north of Chillicothe, Ohio, on Route 104. Marked trails, an observation deck, and a visitor center are also at the site. The park is open 8:00 A.M. to 5:00 P.M. Labor day to mid-June. Summer hours are 8:00 A.M to 8:00 P.M. For more information, write to or call Mound City Group National Monument, 16062 Ohio Route 104, Chillicothe, OH 45601; (614) 774-1125.

Hopewell Ceremonial Mask excavated in Mound City, Ohio.

"The Spirits Were There for Me. . . ."

Vicki has reclaimed her part-Native American roots by becoming a Shawnee ceremonial leader. In preparation for a sunrise ceremony, she went to some of the sites in Ohio for inspiration and received this insight.

"*I stayed in campgrounds not far from the sites. One night I committed to staying up all night, drumming and chanting to ask for guidance. But all I was getting back was the drone from the traffic. I tried harder to concentrate, but just couldn't. It went on all night and I was miserable. Every truck and car was noticeable to me as it roared by. I spent the rest of the night watching the fire from a burnoff stack, which I figured was from a nearby oil refinery. It was up in the sky not too far in the distance. I watched it until sunrise.*

"*After sunrise I packed up and headed for Flint Ridge. I felt awful. I was driving up the road when it occurred to me what I had been given that night. It hit me so powerfully that I pulled over and started crying. What I had been given was the sound of our civilization—our own constant grating noise that's so overwhelming we can't think or hope to escape our ruts. Sound is an instrument, a tool that can heal or hurt. Our society is filled with so much noise, it's one of the ways we're suffocating ourselves, why we're so out of balance. We're completely tone-deaf to the subtleties in life and to the inner voices and spirits that can heal us. And that's what I talked about. That knowledge was my gift.*

"*Later, I tried to find the burnoff stack, but there are none in the area. The spirits were there for me that night. They were the vision of the fire, and I was glad not to have failed them. Even the hardest times can be filled with the greatest lessons.*"

Lizard Mound County Park, Wisconsin

Imagine looking out over an uncultivated field, only a century ago, and seeing nearly a thousand earthworks dotting the landscape. Birds, panthers, reptiles, bears—a veritable grass-covered topiary for the pleasure of the heavens. In between the animals are geometric shapes—cones, circles, lines, and squares—perhaps representing the constellations, charting their movements, recording and predicting seasons and eclipses. Or perhaps they chart the homes of the gods and visitors from the sky.

Ninety-eight percent of the known effigy mounds in the United States, maybe five thousand of them in all, were found in Wisconsin. Lizard Mound County Park, located in southeastern Wisconsin outside of West Bend, features thirty-one effigy mounds. Each of them is three or four feet high and crafted in geometric and animal shapes.

Many of these effigies were used as gravesites. Corpses were often placed at the site of vital organs or, in the case of bird effigies, in the wings. It is speculated that the animal effigy of the grave was the totem of the person buried within and represented him or her. Although these burial sites are similar to those of the Hopewell, their builders did not bury objects along with the bodies. It is hypothesized that they were a splinter group.

To reach **Lizard Mound County Park**, travel 4 miles northeast of West Bend on Route 144. Then drive 1 mile east on County Trunk Highway A to the directional marker. The site is open year-round, except during heavy snows, from 7:00 A.M. to 9:00 P.M. For more information, write to or call Washington County Land Use & Park Department, PO Box 1986, West Bend, WI 53095-7986; (414) 338-4445.

Effigy Mounds National Monument, Iowa

This park contains the vestiges of eighteen hundred years of prehistoric American worship dating from around 500 B.C. to A.D. 1300. The 1,475 acres include 191 "known" mounds, mostly conical or linear in form (the significance of which no one knows), and 29 animal effigies.

Particularly extraordinary is this park's group of effigies called the Marching Bears, sculpted earthworks that represent ten bears in an arc, with three eagles nearby. Each bear is about three feet high and roughly ninety feet long. Two of the large eagles lead the bears, and the other is near the end of the line. The menagerie is followed by two long, linear-shaped mounds. Though the arc and lines that comprise the shape of the entire group seem to resemble a star group, to my knowledge no astronomer has done any testing for possible sky alignments or constellation comparisons.

Also in the park is the Great Bear Mound, 137 feet long and 3½ feet high. The cliffs bordering the park on the east offer beautiful views of the Mississippi River, and there are eleven miles of trails.

Effigy Mounds National Monument is located 3 miles north of Marquette, Iowa on Route 76. The park is open 8:00 A.M. to 7:00 P.M. Memorial Day to Labor Day and 8:00 A.M. to 5:00 P.M. the rest of the year. It is closed Christmas.

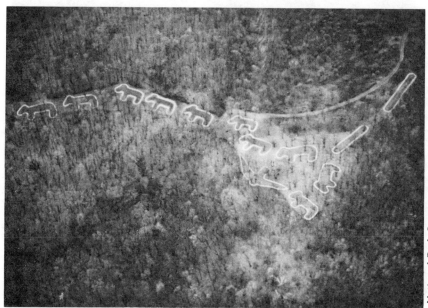

Effigy Mounds National Monument

National Park Service

For more information, write to or call Effigy Mounds National Monument, Harper's Ferry, IA 52146; (319) 873-3491.

Cahokia Mounds Historic Site, Illinois

Though the Hopewell culture began to die out sometime around A.D. 700, the tradition of mound building did not. In fact, it became more magnificent. A new civilization arose, supplanted the Hopewell, and lasted for about eight hundred years. Not knowing what they called themselves, archaeologists labeled them the Mississippian Tradition and Temple Mound Builders, simply because they lived in the valleys of the Mississippi River and many of its tributaries.

This industrious new culture built huge earthworks, sometimes in a pyramidal flat-top shape similar to Mayan

Cahokia Mounds State Historic Site

Cahokia—Monk's Mound

Comparison of the Adena Waverly Tablet and a Mayan tablet representing the jester god. Both dated A.D. 100.

architecture. Mere burial mounds pale by comparison. Also as in the Mayan communities, these earthwork temples were often situated around a plaza, creating a massive ceremonial center. On top of these earthen pyramids, the Mississippians built wooden temples and the houses of priests and chieftains. From the top, you can look around and experience the breathtaking 360-degree view they enjoyed.

The Temple Mound Builders were prodigious farmers, hunters, and artisans. They were also furious organizers held together by a complicated social structure and, in their later days, the brutal Buzzard Cult religion. The culture appears to have begun along the Mississippi River in Illinois, and spread as far north as Wisconsin and as far south as Florida.

The suspicion that the Mayans influenced Hopewell and even the earlier Adena cultures is mostly a matter of conjecture. There is no doubt, however, that there was strong Mayan and other Mesoamerican influence on the Mississippians, as well as other North American peoples such as the Anasazi of the Southwest.

Painting by William R. Iseminger

Cahokia in A.D. 1200.

The Mississippian Tradition took shape and prospered at the same time Classic Mayan culture began to fall apart in Mexico, from roughly A.D. 800 to 900. Nothing specific tells of a large migration into the area; nevertheless, the similarities between the two cultures are too remarkable to be dismissed easily.

Latter Mississippian culture degenerated into grisly religious practices involving ceremonial human sacrifice and cannibalism at roughly the same time as the Mayan Revival (about A.D. 1150 to 1400) centered in Mexico's Yucatan Peninsula. The Mayans were then under the rule of the bloodthirsty Toltecs. Wide-scale ritual sacrifice and cannibalism were an omnipresent feature of the Mayan Revival, as they were under the Aztecs, who would rise to preeminence in central Mexico toward the end of this era. Evidently, these practices spread northward along the trade routes.

Besides the clear similarity of Mississippian and Mayan urban planning, there were also similarities in dress, worship, and science. Found in the ruins of the Mississippians' culture were artifacts featuring winged serpents, the symbol of the Mayan god Kukulcan (later known as Quetzalcoatl). Legend has it that Kukulcan brought architecture, astronomy, writing, and religion to a previously uncivilized people. Other items unearthed in the temple mounds have included ear spools, double-bladed knives and swords used for religious purposes, artworks, pottery, and decorated conch shells.

These Mississippian artworks often feature wild and fantastic scenes, disembodied human parts, weeping eyes, and creepy animalistic creatures. The meaning of these symbols has been lost. All of these were products of the Southern Buzzard Cult period, which exhibited an extravagant and neurotic preoccupation with the other side.

It was the Spanish explorer Hernando de Soto who set the precedent for dealing with Native Americans when he marched through what is now the southeastern United States for three years beginning in 1539. De Soto's bloody campaign is known as "The Trail of Tears." Mercilessly, he ordered the arms of scores of captured people cut off, then forced his mutilated prisoners to march in chains in front of his forces in order to intimidate the populace. Although some mound building was reported to be going on at the time, de Soto's march depleted native food supplies and spread diseases unknown in the New World.

But even before de Soto's arrival, something catastrophic had happened to the Mississippians in the fourteenth century. Cahokia, the largest city, was abandoned by 1500. The remnants of the once mighty Mississippian Temple Mound Builders were dying off or had disintegrated into smaller tribes. Like the Classic Mayans, who disappeared in the ninth century, like the Anasazi and Hohokam of the Southwest, the Mississippians' end remains a mystery. De Soto may simply have finished off a dying culture. The Spaniards' devastation surely spread panic and might have broken the survivors spiritually. Whatever actually happened, the remnants of the once-magnificent Mound Builders crumbled into the landscape to spawn the tribes of the Northeast, the plains, and the South, leaving behind the remains of their sacred past.

The greatest ceremonial center of the Mississippians was Cahokia, which once supported a community of some forty thousand. The remains of this once grand city survives about thirty miles outside of East St. Louis, Illinois.

Cahokia was the religious and trade center, the Tibet and Chicago rolled into one, during the centuries of vibrant Mississippian civilization. Situated near the confluence of two great rivers—the Mississippi and the Missouri—Cahokia was the heart of prehistoric America for almost a thousand years. What the inhabitants called this splendid city is unknown. The name Cahokia derives from a tribe found

Cahokia Mounds—Excavations

living near the site several hundred years after the fall. Nevertheless, the influence of this remarkable place stretched across the length and breadth of half a continent. Cahokia was the vortex.

Though the city appears to have been inhabited first by offshoots from the Hopewell culture as early as A.D. 700, the Mississippians who settled in the area around A.D. 900 radically improved the temple mounds. They didn't live in teepees or huts, but rather thatched-roof cabins with clay-plastered walls. The city covered six square miles, with houses surrounding central plazas. It also had suburban residential areas. There were agricultural fields as well as home gardens.

A couple of hundred years later, Cahokia became stratified into social classes, and a wall was built around the central sacred area; either to protect it or to separate the priests and kings, whose homes were often built on top of the mounds from the people.

Unlike with the Adena and Hopewell, just a few of the mounds were used as sacred gravesites. The mounds apparently were used more for elevating religious ceremonies, bringing them closer to the sky and farther away from the noise of the city.

The grounds of Cahokia are vast. They include eighty-seven mounds, a village and other reconstructions, and a pathway to the top of the enormous Monks Mound. A lovely museum displays much of what has been uncovered in archaeological excavations of the grounds. Should you visit, there are three Cahokian features not to be missed:

Monks Mound

Monks Mound is the largest known earthwork in the Western Hemisphere. If you visit Cahokia, you couldn't miss it if you tried. Its base covers fourteen acres, and it rises in four platform terraces to a height of a hundred feet. Eight centuries ago it was probably much higher. The chief lived on top in a temple. To give you an idea of how huge it is, four thousand people gathered on top of it for a Native American ceremony on the Harmonic Convergence, August 16-17, 1987. The massive construction was named Monks Mound because a group of Jesuits lived on top of it for a while. Interesting that they should have been so attracted to its energy.

Mound 72

Despite its terribly drab name (the Cahokia staff should hold a Rename Mound 72 Contest), Mound 72 was the site of a chilling yet extravagant mass grave, possible evidence of the later Buzzard Cult religion of the Temple Mound Builders. Furthermore, the mound's ridgetop appears to be sky-aligned with the winter solstice sunrise. Found during excavations of the mound were three hundred burials, primarily young women, and the grave of a God King, whose skeleton lay on a blanket of twenty thousand shell beads. The king was surrounded by sacrificed servants and offerings, including eight hundred arrowheads made of different colors and materials. Another part of the mound contained the bones of four men with their heads and hands missing. Still another yielded the skeletons of fifty-three women. Was it simply the honored women's burial ground? Did they die of one of the many speculated diseases that ravaged their society and caused its demise? Or were they sacrificed per the dictates of their religion?

Woodhenge

The three astronomically aligned circles dubbed Woodhenge were discovered and later reconstructed by archaeologist Warren Wittry in the early sixties. He and his team were doing salvage archaeology (that is, "Let's salvage what we can before the bulldozers come in") prior to the construction of Interstate 55-70. Wittry's sensitive eyes recognized deep soil stains—the footprints, if you will, of an ancient cedar construction. What they had uncovered was

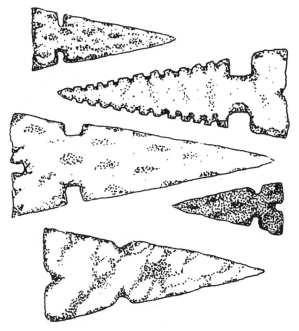

Arrowheads from Cahokia Mounds.

once three wooden circles most likely used for calendrical and astronomical purposes.

Some scientists consider Cahokia's Woodhenge even more astronomically accurate than England's famous Stonehenge. One of the circles has a carbon date of A.D. 815, predating the height of Cahokian civilization by three hundred years. Astronomically oriented programs are featured at Woodhenge at sunrise throughout the year.

To see Cahokia, first of all, don't confuse it with the town of Cahokia, which is south of East St. Louis. The Cahokia Mounds State Historic Site is in Collinsville, Illinois. Echoing its olden days, Cahokia is a big and busy place with a large, dedicated staff, volunteers, and park rangers. They sponsor archaeological classes, digs, and trips to nearby sites. They also publish their own newsletter and promote Native American traditions through arts and crafts classes, storytelling days, and other delightful programs.

Cahokia Mounds Historic Site can be reached by taking Exit 6 off Interstate 55-70 to Route 111 south. Then go east on U.S. 40 to the Cahokia Mounds. There are signs leading to the mounds beginning on the Interstate. The site is open 8:00 A.M. to dusk daily. Closed on major holidays. For more information, write to or call Cahokia Mounds State Historic Site, PO Box 681, Collinsville, IL 62234; (618) 344-5268.

Aztalan Mound Park, Wisconsin

"We are determined to preserve these ruins from being ruined." So wrote archaeologist Nathaniel Hyer in 1837, two years after the site was discovered near Lake Mills, Wisconsin. It was Hyer who named Aztalan, citing its Mexican influence. Yet despite his fierce determination, a year later the government sold the land upon which Aztalan stood for $22.

The awesome ancient city that consisted of three pyramid earthworks, numerous houses, a stockade wall, burial grounds, and intricate artifacts was leveled and hauled away.

For the next 130 years, dedicated people continued to fight to save this sacred site, starting with three acres that contained eight of the original seventy-four mounds. It finally became a National Historic Landmark in 1964 and included 120 acres of the original land. Since that time, archaeologists and other groups have painstakingly excavated the land and reconstructed the original pyramids and stockade wall. The battle to save Aztalan is a modern sacred site fable.

Aztalan was built and occupied from about A.D. 1100 to 1300. A stockaded village, it was inhabited by about five hundred people who migrated into the area, most likely from Cahokia. It is considered to be the northernmost outpost of the Mississippian Temple Mound Builders. Judging from its charred remains, the community's end came when it was burned down, either during an attack by the surrounding Woodland people, who resented the superior intruders, or by accident. Common to the culture of all temple mound sites, Aztalan's recovered artworks and implements are lavish. A crematorium has also been excavated.

Probably the most sensational find at Aztalan is the "Princess" burial. Deep within a burial mound, the skeleton of a young woman was discovered. She was twenty to twenty-five years of age when she died, five feet, seven inches tall, and was wrapped in three strands of 1,978 shell beads. The beads, some of which were individually shaped, are thought to be from Gulf Coast shells. The princess now resides in the archives of the Milwaukee Public Museum.

Aztalan State Park and Museum are located 3 miles east of Lake Mills, Wisconsin, on County Road Q, south of County Road B. The park is open daylight hours April through October. For more information, write or call Aztalan c/o 2405 Door Creek Road, Stoughton, WI 53589; (608) 873-9695.

SOUTHEAST

5
THE SOUTHEAST:
THE MISSISSIPPIANS AND
THE BUZZARD CULT

The Southeast holds a wealth of sacred sites occupied by Native American societies centuries before Columbus. In this region of the U.S. you'll find enigmatic petroglyphs, the remains of awe-inspiring mound cities, rejuvenating hot springs, and compelling evidence of ancient travel to and from the Yucatan Peninsula.

Town Creek Indian Mound, North Carolina

Closer to us in time than most of the other Mississippian societies, Town Creek in North Carolina has given us a glimpse into the rich lives of its splendid earlier inhabitants.

Town Creek was an exclusive ceremonial center and contained within its walls temples, a game court, sacred councils, and burial grounds. Built like a stockade, it housed only priests. The Creek Indians drove out the previous Siouan residents (not to be confused with the Sioux) and made Town Creek their own from roughly A.D. 1450 to 1650. Then the Siouans returned to reclaim their land and drive out the Creek. People from the region would gather for holidays, sports and games, funerals for their leaders, and religious ceremonies. The last included both long fasts and purification rites as well as feasts.

One of their most important holidays was the Ceremony of the Busk, or Fast, an eight-day celebration in which the inhabitants marked their new year by breaking the fast with the ritual eating of new corn. A cleansing and fresh start was proclaimed for the entire community. Houses and grounds were cleaned and repaired, problems were solved, and all crimes except murder were forgiven. Murder was handled between the offender's and the victim's family, either by paying damages or by exacting revenge, a life for a life.

Sports events, in which warriors from different villages would form teams and compete, were also held in the plaza. They played a strenuous ball game that had elements of both football and lacrosse. Like today, competing in these ball games was one of the ways a man could gain prestige in society.

The main thatched-roof temple, now reconstructed, sat on top of an earthen pyramidal mound. Situated before its ramp were four huts that surrounded the most sacred plot of ground. Here is where the *talwa* or soul of the community was thought to reside. On this plot, the chiefs gathered to discuss and make decisions affecting community affairs. Though class-structured and ruled by their priests and chiefs, their government and ethics of responsibility and sharing were exemplary compared to those of many contemporary governments.

The Creeks were sun worshipers and kept sacred eternal fires. Surrounding the fire were four logs that, as in so many other religions, marked the four directions.

Though the Creek culture was an unusual combination of ancient Mississippian and contemporary Native American ways, the demise of the Creek also meant the end of any knowledge of them until archaeologists began to excavate Town Creek earlier this century.

Town Creek Indian Mound is located off Route 73 on tiny Route 3 near Mt. Gilead. It is open year-round and closes at dusk. For more information, write to or call Town Creek State Historic Site, Route 3, Box 50, Mt. Gilead, NC 27306; (919) 439-6802.

Judaculla Rock, North Carolina

After you have visited Town Creek, should you find yourself near Asheville, North Carolina, it is worthwhile to ride down to Cullowhee, known primarily for Western Carolina University.

In the vicinity is a stunning flat-surfaced soapstone boulder about fourteen feet across. Called Judaculla Rock, this petroglyph is totally covered with wild and frenzied ancient markings. To this day, it is a complete enigma, its artist unknown and its designs indecipherable.

Some of the designs include seven-fingered hands, arrows, stick figures, concentric circles, hieroglyphiclike figures, and various other symbols.

There is no telling how old Judaculla Rock may be. It definitely predates the arrival of colonists to the area over 250 years ago and may be older than the Cherokee nation. Though they lay no claim to having created it, the Rock does figure prominently in Cherokee legends.

Judaculla was a tremendous giant, combination Cyclops and Paul Bunyan, who protected the animals and birds of the forest. His father was thunder, his mother a blazing comet, and he was so big he could step from mountain to mountain and drink a steam dry. He left his marks on Judaculla Rock when he jumped from the mountaintop into Caney Fork Creek. Some say that the markings were Judaculla's laws of the hunt, which instructed hunters to take no more game than needed, so to preserve the forest for all time.

Judaculla Rock was also a peace treaty marker and meeting place for whites and Indians. It was purchased by Jackson County in 1959 from the private landowner to keep it from being weathered and destroyed.

The Judaculla Rock petroglyphs suggest so much to the

imagination. Still, we are buffeted by the cold wind of the unknown, wondering who left us these messages and what we were meant to know.

To reach **Judaculla Rock**, travel $3\frac{1}{2}$ miles south out of Cullowhee on Route 107, then go east on Caney Fork Road for 3 miles. For more information, write to or call the Jackson County Chamber of Commerce, 18 North Central Street, Sylva, NC 28779; (704) 586-2155.

Crystal River State Archaeological Site, Florida

For sixteen centuries beginning around 200 B.C., generation after generation of ancient Floridians lived, played, worked, worshiped, fell in love, and enjoyed the sunshine and warm waters of a place known today as the Crystal River State Archaeological Site. They were lucky folk, for Crystal River was and still is an inspiring and appealing place.

This age-old site, located along the sparkling Crystal River not far from the Gulf of Mexico, was inhabited by all of the mound-building cultures. It flourished until about A.D. 1400, when its occupants, like the inhabitants of so many other pre-Columbian settlements, mysteriously vanished.

Judging from what was left behind, it appears that the people of the Crystal River mounds were important instructors for more northern communities. Pyramidal earthworks were built at Crystal River long before they were engineered by the Hopewellian and Mississippian communities of Illinois and Ohio. Trade routes into the heartland of ancient America were well worn. Shell ornaments from Florida and the Gulf of Mexico have been discovered up and down the Mississippi River basin. Excavated artifacts from this important Florida center include flint knives from the Ohio Valley.

Similar to Poverty Point, Louisiana (described later in this chapter), Crystal River appears to have been a traveler's way station for ideas and people travelling to and from the Yucatan Peninsula.

Two stone slabs unearthed at Crystal River are particularly significant. Called *stelae*, the slabs are remarkably similar to others found by the hundreds throughout overgrown and abandoned Mayan cities in Mexico, Guatemala, and Honduras. These stone stelae were public monuments for the Mayans, on which were recorded significant historical events and precise dates in the most advanced written language ever developed in ancient America. However, the stelae at Crystal River exhibit faces, not writing.

Other artifacts display the march of time and progress in the city over hundreds of years. These include ceramic goods, shell ornaments and jewelry, rock crystal necklaces and pendants, ear spools, copper goods, weapons, and tools.

Crystal River has two temple mounds, including one 235 feet long, two burial mounds from which 450 skeletons have been excavated, and two middens, or refuse mounds.

Mississippian Symbols—Suns, lightning, weeping eye.

At Crystal River, they consist primarily of discarded seafood shells. There is also an astronomical observatory constructed of shell and stone that has been proven to track solar movements precisely. The stelae are also part of this astronomical system.

The once-influential city has been designated as an archaeological site since 1903 but has yet to be entirely excavated.

The area is a natural ecological center. Hordes of Florida's precious St. Bernards of the water, the gentle manatees, gather there in winter, as do many exotic species of birds and animals. Standing amid the tropical splendor, it is easy to understand why more than modern-day snowbirds have been attracted to Florida's rejuvenating climes. For those who want to dance with the manatees, there is scuba diving along the river.

Crystal River State Archaeological Site is located about 75 miles north of Tampa, Florida, in Crystal River off U.S. 19. Take the State Park Road off ramp and travel west 2½ miles. The grounds are open seven days a week from 8:00 A.M. to sunset. The museum is open Thursday through Monday from 9:00 A.M. to 5:00 P.M. There are a number of self-guided trails. For more information, write to or call Crystal River State Archaeological Site, 3400 North Museum Point, Crystal River, FL 32629; (904) 795-3817.

"Our Bodies Felt Transparent"

Diane is a yoga teacher, artist, and mother of four from Tampa, Florida. She went to Crystal River for an afternoon jaunt with two friends, Barbara, an astrologer who works for the FBI, and Pat, a geologist from Seattle.

"It was a very auspicious time for a visit to a sacred site. Astrologically, Uranus and Saturn were conjunct to each other. It was a gorgeous day, just beautiful. It's a very peaceful spot, and you can feel the energy everywhere. It caresses you like soft kisses. The feeling there is one of ecology and balance, very healing and nurturing.

"We visited the different earthworks and climbed to the top of the temple mound and meditated. It was windy and brisk on top. We could look out over the Crystal River. The river really shines; it looks like crystal and glistens and gleams in the sunlight. We all had different sensations of the place, and each one of us was unaware what the others were sensing. Pat smelled burning wood from a campfire from the northwest direction. Barbara kept hearing a birdsong that got closer and closer until she thought it was in front of her, but when she opened her eyes there was nothing there. The sensation for me was vibration in the air like a light tapping or brushing against your skin.

"As we walked around, we began to feel a little dizzy, even punchy. It was hard for us to completely walk straight. I can't explain it. The pull of gravity is different there. There's less pull. We were tripping over our own feet, and it really made us laugh. It was as though the air was so refined we had to rethink our walking and being upright. It was marvelous, though, and we felt great— almost walking without our feet touching the ground. And our bodies felt transparent. We could feel the energy going through us, in and then out again, not just around us. It was a very strong force. Quite thrilling."

Etowah Mounds State Historic Site, Georgia

Should you visit Etowah, climb the stairway to the top of Mound A (another terrible name), which is about six stories high. Here you can share the view Etowah's chiefs and priests had six hundred years ago. Here you can look down upon the ceremonial plaza made of packed red clay. To the east are the Altoona Mountains over which the sun rises and to the west the Etowah River and Pumpkinvine Creek. The atmosphere here is quiet but vibrant, if for no other reason than that this great temple mound has never been excavated. In fact, only 8 percent of Etowah has been excavated. As one Georgia lady told me, "It's a very spiritual place. When I was a young girl, I used to ride my horse around the village. The horse would just bring itself here. She loved it. I've been coming here my whole life, and I never get tired of it. Just the opposite in fact. It always makes me feel good."

Situated next to the river, this once vital ceremonial center is now serene but still beautiful. The temple mound is the second largest after Monks Mound at Cahokia and contains 4.3 million cubic feet of earth. Similar to Cahokia, Etowah was inhabited for nearly a thousand years, from A.D. 700 to 1600. People from all over the river valley gathered for religious festivals at the ceremonial plaza beneath the great temple that stood on top of its earthen pyramid. Surrounding the fortified city of several thousand people was a ditch twelve feet deep and twice as wide.

Although later Etowah culture, around A.D. 1500, would most probably have been involved in the Buzzard Cult, none of the excavations have revealed anything of significance regarding what might have been frequent ritual sacrifice. Archaeologists, however, in their studies and excavations of about five hundred burials at Etowah, were stunned by the lavishness of the clothing and artifacts discovered in the graves of the chiefs. Included were two statues of a man and a woman carved from blocks of Georgia marble. These wonderful statues are on display at the site.

Marble man and woman statues from Etowah burial mounds dated A.D. 1400.

The **Etowah Mounds State Historic Site** is northeast of Atlanta. They can be reached by taking Georgia State Route 113/61 south out of Cartersville and exiting onto Etowah Mounds Road into the site. The site is open year-round, Tuesday through Saturday, 9:00 A.M. to 5:00 P.M., and Sunday afternoons. For more information, write to or call Etowah Mound State Historic Site, Route 2, Cartersville, GA 30120; (404) 387-3747.

Rock Eagle Effigy, Georgia

In the cool earth of northern Georgia, a soaring eagle made of white quartz stones, with a wingspan of 120 feet, stands in timeless, mute testimony of an ancient people. Eagles and other kinds of birds figured strongly in mound-building cultures as well as in the lore of more modern Native

American tribes. Sculpted earthworks of birds have been found in Iowa, Wisconsin, Ohio, and Louisiana, as well as Georgia. It is no mistake that the great American bald eagle is our symbol. It was also the symbol of the great Iroquois Confederacy. With the freedom of flight, the great birds were believed to bridge the gap between our reality and the other side, ushering souls after death to their home in the heavens. Moreover, they were a symbol of strength, vision, and wisdom, garnered from their proximity to the Great Spirit in the skies overhead.

It is possible that the Rock Eagle Effigy was used in religious ceremonies 6,000 years ago. What these ceremonies may have been like boggles the imagination.

As at the Great Serpent Mound in Ohio (see Chapter 4) a tower has been built so the Eagle can be seen, as it should be, from the air.

The **Rock Eagle Effigy** is located in northern Georgia, 7 miles north of Eatonton, off U.S. 441. This sacred site is on the grounds of a 1,500-acre state conference center used by many 4-H clubs, which include campgrounds. The Effigy is open daylight hours year round. Nearby is another similar eagle effigy that is, unfortunately, not open to the public. For more information, write to or call Rock Eagle State 4-H Club Center, U.S. 441, Eatonton, GA 31024; (404) 485-2831.

Mound State Monument, Alabama

Situated on the banks of the Black Warrior River, Mound State Monument is one of the most beautifully preserved and lovely mound city sites. Similar to Cahokia and Town Creek, the Native Americans who lived here were part of the later Mississippian culture.

Mound State Monument covers 320 acres and includes twenty pyramidal and oval mounds, including a large ceremonial earthwork about six stories high with a reconstructed wooden temple on top. A graded stairway leads to the top. Archaeologists estimate there were three thousand permanent residents at Moundville, although many people living in the surrounding areas probably gathered there for sacred ceremonies, games, and holidays. Moundville was undoubtedly the main government and ceremonial center for the entire region.

At the museum, one can clearly see the influence that the advanced Meso-American empires had on the architecture, dress, and artworks left by these ancient Alabamians. One cannot help feeling a deep appreciation for this very sophisticated society that flourished and developed on American soil for centuries, then confoundingly disappeared.

Moundville, Alabama

Alabama State Museum of Natural History

Mound State Monument lies off Route 69, 15 miles south of Tuscaloosa. It is now part of the University of Alabama. It is open year-round, 9:00 A.M. to 5:00 P.M. (closed Christmas and Thanksgiving) and there are camping facilities on the site. For more information, write to or call Mound State Monument, PO Box 66, Moundville, AL 35474; (205) 371-2572.

Poverty Point, Louisiana

In 1953, a sharp employee of the Department of the Army noticed something strange about the land along the Bayou Macon in an aerial photograph taken by the mapmaking division. What he noticed were a group of unnatural-looking earth forms and low-lying ridges a mile long that stretched across the northern Louisiana landscape not far from the

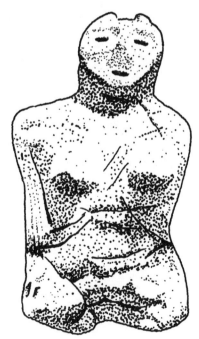

Female figure from Poverty Point. Evidence of Goddess and nature worship.

banks of Bayou Macon near the Mississippi. More photos and further investigation confirmed what he had already suspected—he had found the remnants of an ancient city.

Poverty Point is one of the oldest cities ever discovered on our continent. It parallels and may even predate the Adena and Hopewell cultures. There is now evidence supporting the idea that it was built by the first community of Mayans to migrate into North America from Mexico. As it is, the mouth of the Mississippi lies directly across the gulf from the Yucatan Peninsula.

The name of this fabulous site is a real misnomer. Poverty Point does not refer to the wealthy civilization that flourished in northeastern Louisiana some thirty-five centuries ago. Rather, it refers to the antebellum cotton plantation that was built on the land ages later.

The trade routes from other mound cities were well established. Artifacts unearthed here have included flint from Ohio, slate and copper from the Great Lakes, and soapstone from Appalachia. Numerous clay female figurines have been excavated there, as well as fired-clay balls that substituted for stones in the soft, stoneless Louisiana landscape. Millions of these clay balls have been found indicating the place supported at different times a very large population. Archaeologists are just beginning to tap the wonders of Poverty Point.

Most stunning, however, are the mounds themselves. Engineered in six concentric half-octagons like an amphitheater, they were carefully constructed to permit observation of spring and fall equinox sunrises. The entire complex measures three-quarters of a mile across. All the ridges together comprise about eleven miles of mound building— a herculean task even today.

A startling mound in the shape of a bird displays an outstretched wingspan of 640 feet. This magnificent Bird Mound stands seven stories high just west of the complex. Many bird artifacts have also been found at Poverty Point.

Furthermore, the aisles between the mound sections are aligned to the summer and winter solstices. Little more is known for sure. The mysteries hang heavy over this site. Like the earthworks of Newark, Ohio (see Chapter 4), the octagon shapes of Poverty Point must mean something. The veil, however, is yet to be pulled back.

Poverty Point is located 5 miles outside Epps, Louisiana. You can reach the site by driving Route 134 east from Epps and 1 mile north on Route 577. It is open year-round except for holidays Wednesday–Sunday 9:00 A.M. to 5:00 P.M. For more information, write to or call Poverty Point State Commemorative Area, Box 208-A, Epps, LA 71237; (318) 926-5492.

Hot Springs National Park, Arkansas

Welcome to hot springs happiness. Pure, cleansing, and healing, hot springs are enormously regenerative to our bodies and our spirits. All people, ancient and modern, have found renewal in their soothing waters.

There are over a hundred natural hot springs in the United States. Due to their enduring popularity, it is difficult, though not impossible, to find a hot spring today in its original, untouched setting. The waters of most of them are no longer open-air, but covered and rerouted into nearby bathhouses.

There are excellent reasons for this. Above all, it protects the spring's waters from mixing with pollutants from automobiles or contaminated rainwater. Certainly, it would be more exciting to experience a hot spring in all its raw integrity, bubbling from the deep, misting the air, surrounded by glistening rocks covered with soft blue-green moss. But it is a necessary compromise. Though the water may not be as aesthetically pleasing surrounded by tile and beach chairs, it is all the more pure. Relax and enjoy it, because there's not much else to do anyway. It's hot springs Zen.

Most American hot springs are located along the Appalachian Mountains, in the Rockies, or west of them. Oddly enough, one of the largest enclaves is in the middle of the country: Arkansas. Hot Springs, Arkansas, is world-famous for its healing waters. Forty-seven of them lie close to the most crystal-laden mountains in North America. Hot Springs National Park offers eleven miles of shady trails that wind their way through hills streaked with crystal quartz and other minerals. Although the spring area now looks dramatically different than it did a hundred years ago, it is fortunately protected from overdevelopment by its natural condition. Further construction would ruin the springs and cause the mountains literally to crumble.

Native Americans from different tribes went to the springs for healing. For them the springs embodied the nurturing of the Great Spirit/Mother Earth partnership. It was revered land, and the rejuvenation received from the springs was readily acknowledged through ceremony and offerings.

It was also a peaceful land. It is noteworthy that despite the hostility among various tribes in the region, the springs were democratically declared a neutral zone, to be shared equally among all. In this sacred place people worshiped as one. They called the springs Medicine Waters, referring not only to their healing properties but to their spiritual proper-ties as well, *medicine* connoting "spirit." So it was for hundreds of years.

There is some evidence that de Soto and his army went to the springs. It is said that, hearing of the magical waters, de Soto thought he may have discovered the Fountain of Youth that Ponce de Leon died searching for. Yet when he came upon the miraculous Valley of the Vapors, possibly in the winter of 1541, he was disappointed by the hot springs and steaming mud holes. He explained to the people that his disease could be cured only by gold. He spent the next month resupplying his army, then pressed on to the Missis-sippi River and went south. He died a few months later.

The hot springs remained in native hands over the next three hundred years, although they were often visited by European trappers, traders, plantation owners, and other white folks in the know. In 1804, Thomas Jefferson sent out an exploration party to find out exactly what the Louisiana Purchase included. Their glowing report about the springs did not go unheeded. In 1832, Andrew Jackson took formal government possession of Hot Springs, which was followed by rapid development. By the early twentieth century, Hot Springs was an elegant resort featuring the luxurious Bath House Row. In 1921, Hot Springs and its adjacent mountains were declared a national park.

Today Hot Springs is part resort town and part protected parkland. Ten of the five thousand acres comprising the park feature the springs. Forty-five of these are now capped and routed underground to surrounding bathing areas and drinking fountains, supplying about 850,000 gallons of springwater a day. Though water from a hot spring often comes from underground rivers, in Hot Springs National Park you are getting rainwater that has been processed meticulously underground for four thousand years. The temperature from some of the springs is as high as 143 degrees. Two of them are still open-air and displayed.

To say the area is rich in gems and minerals is an understatement. Arkansas, in particular the Ouachita River region, which includes Hot Springs, is the crystal center of North America. The crystals here are famed for their superior brilliance. A. Van Cleef wrote about the spectacular crystals in an article, "The Hot Springs of Arkansas," published in Harper's in 1878:

> On the hillsides near the hot springs beautiful clear quartz crystals are found lying among the grass blades. . . . The famed "Crystal Mountain" is some thirty miles from the springs, but at different localities in the vicinity of the town fine masses of pure white translucent quartz crystals can be found incrusting fissures in the rocks. From the Crystal Mountain and other crystal mines nearer the springs, the "crystal hunters" as they are called, bring in wagonloads of magnificent specimens. Some of the blocks, glittering with thousands of various-sized pointed hexagonal prisms, are as large as two or three feet square.

The region is also famous for its novaculite or Arkansas stone. Used by Native Americans for arrowheads, it is still mined and exported worldwide as whetstone. An ancient novaculite quarry can be seen in the park high on Indian Mountain. It is approximately 150 feet wide and 25 feet deep. There are also many other types of precious stones besides crystal quartz at Hot Springs, including agate, garnets, mica, and other minerals.

Also featured high on a ridge is an enigmatic balanced rock. A true megalithic mystery, this huge boulder stands precariously perched on a fingerlike mountain ledge.

Hot Springs is a sacred site ideally designed for healing, rest, and renewal.

Hot Springs National Park is located in central Arkansas off Route 7. The visitor center is located in downtown Hot Springs. The park is open year-round, 8:00 A.M. to 5:00 P.M. For more information, write to or call Hot Springs National Park; PO Box 1860, Hot Springs National Park, AR 71902; (501) 624-3383.

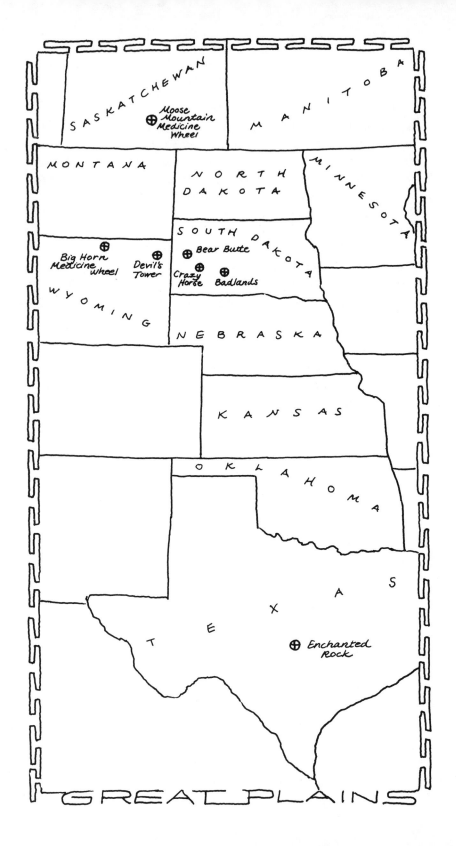

GREAT PLAINS

6
THE GREAT PLAINS: SACRED LANDS AND MEDICINE WHEELS

To visit the sacred sites of the Great Plains is to steep yourself in the history of the Native Americans of the region. To those who have opened themselves to the area's power, these sites hold great spiritual significance and exude a fierce energy. It can be felt in the astounding mountains and caves provided by the Earth herself as well as in the human-made structures left for us to decipher. The medicine wheels of the northern plains are a notable feature; perhaps through your own experiences there you can help to unravel their mysteries.

Enchanted Rock, Texas

Enchanted Rock is a billion years old. Located in central Texas, it is a gigantic mass of pink granite that sparkles in the moonlight after the rain and makes strange, crackling sounds at night. As fantastic as that may seem, it is not what makes Enchanted Rock a sacred site.

For thousands of years it has been a holy mountain for people near and far, having been worshiped by succeeding

Ira Kennedy

Enchanted Rock

generations of Native Americans and inspiring many tales. It was, and still is, believed to be a doorway to the spirit world. Native shamans and medicine men would gather there to practice their magic and meet with the other side. Young men often used Enchanted Rock as the site of their first solo vision quest, which was part of their initiation for becoming warriors.

The holy spirit of the mountain know as Gahe to the Kiowa and Gan to the Apache, was sent by the Great Spirit to teach people a better way to live.

Texas writer and artist Ira Kennedy writes in *The Story-tellers* of an Apache shaman who alerts a few young Comanche ruffians to the sacred land they have come upon. His words embody the spirit of both Enchanted Rock and the vision quest:

"Then join us," the Comanche said. "Honor us with an understanding of this holy mountain."

"So be it," the old man replied. "You ask about the Gahe of the enchanted rock. You want to know what Gahe knows. To do so you must listen to the mountain spirit and not to men. What you hear from men are stories, and what you learn from the mountain is sacred. Stories can be lost, but Gahe lives forever in the mountain's caves."

Most of Texas's Native Americans were forced out of the state a hundred years ago. Nevertheless, their spirits, and Gahe, live on, and the power of Enchanted Rock endures.

Geologically, Enchanted Rock is referred to as an *inselberg*, or an island mountain. Although it is the largest granite dome in the area, other masses appear nearby that are all part of the Enchanted Rock batholith, or a granite mountain range uncovered by erosion. Besides the rock itself, the area features many weirdly shaped granite formations that add to the special feeling of the place. Despite the rugged landscape, the park is quite rich, with over five hundred types of plants and animals. The streaks of water runoff on the rocks are called by legend "trails of molten silver tears."

Archaeological remains indicate that people have gathered in the area for ten thousand years. Yet, despite all this prehistory, the discovery of Enchanted Rock is credited to a Captain Brown in 1829. Passing from owner to owner into this century, Enchanted Rock is fortunately now part of a 1,643-acre preserve operated by Texas Parks and Wildlife in conjunction with the privately funded Nature Conservancy.

Enchanted Rock State Natural Area is in southcentral Texas. Located on Ranch Road 965, it can be found approximately 16 miles north of Fredericksburg. From Llano, take Route 16 south 14 miles, turn right on Ranch Road 965, and drive 8 miles south. There is one campground with facilities and three primitive camping areas. Calling ahead for camping reservations is advised. The park is open year round. For more information, write to or call Enchanted Rock State Natural Area, Route 4, Box 170, Fredericksburg, TX 78624; (915) 247-3903

"A Huge Eagle Wavered over Me."

(Jorge is a Hispanic/Indian who currently conducts Native American sweat lodge ceremonies, a cleansing and meditation ritual, under the guidance of a medicine man. Recovering his Native American roots, he did his first vision quest two years ago with a Lakota guide and tells of his experiences here.)

"My first night was very beautiful. I didn't sleep at all but just stared at the sky and heard all the sounds. I realized we are all relatives across the planet, not just people, but the animals and plants too, and the Earth itself is a living thing. And then I realized that God is both the male and the female aspect of life, and I felt for that union. It was like a communion.

"The second night was the longest night of dreams. My whole life and all my conflicts were appearing in them. But what I learned the night before stayed alive. Past and future came together.

"By the third night I was in terrible pain, and I couldn't sleep at all. It was like it was too much. It was then I had the vision. I knew it was a vision and not a dream because I was awake. I saw myself dancing the Sun Dance. I was in the circle with many other Sun Dancers. I could hear the music and was doing it like I had known it my whole life even though I had never done it before. A huge eagle wavered over me. It wasn't real. It was like a cloud, a spirit eagle, and it was so large.

"The next morning I told the guide, who is a Lakota, what happened to me. I described the Sun Dance as I had visioned it, and he said, 'Yes, that is it.' I told him I wanted to go with him to do the Sun Dance that year. He said I would need preparation, that I wasn't ready. I asked again. Finally he said he would take me, but it would be up to the chief. When we arrived, the chief just looked at me for a long time and said, 'He's ready.'

"I did the Sun Dance. It was like nothing that can be described. It is so much more powerful. After the vision quest, there were so many changes in my life, so fast, it was like being thrown into a frying pan and running around so you didn't get burned. Nothing was the same after it, but everything was better."

The Badlands, South Dakota

The Badlands are a natural testament to the power of the elements. This geological wonderland provides us with a long-term sense of the Earth's restlessness over time. Wind and rain have eroded the rocky landscape of the Badlands into a spectacular display of crests, ridges, buttes, and ravines. The gray and white hues of the sediment from which they are sculpted are threaded with colorful minerals.

The land itself is spare, more rock and grassland than tall tress and verdant hills. But to the Native Americans who continue to live among the craggy outcrops, it is known as a land of extraordinary spiritual power. Named by French-Canadian fur trappers who obviously found the area frustrating, the Badlands are home to prairie dogs, bighorn sheep, coyote, and badgers. An antelopelike animal called the *pronghorn* also abounds, as well as bison, golden eagles, cottontails, deer, and rattlesnakes. If you're lucky, you may see a pronghorn, which can travel up to sixty miles an hour, on the run.

The Badlands once also sported elk, wolves, and bears, but they died out in the last century's migration and gold rushes. So did the bison, which until the mid-nineteenth century roamed the Badlands in the millions, covering acres of land at a time like a huge, dark blanket. The National Park Service has reintroduced bison into the Badlands, and today there are about five hundred of them.

As the land weathered down over the centuries, remarkable fossil beds of the long-gone Oligocene Epoch, among

South Dakota Division of Tourism

The Badlands

South Dakota Division of Tourism

The Badlands

the richest in the world, became uncovered. What has been revealed is a microcosm of planetary evolution. As told by the fossils, thirty million years ago a surprising menagerie wandered through the Badlands. In what is now a land of severe winter, camels once kept guard against saber-toothed tigers, while three-toed horses galloped past woolly mammoths and sloths. During that time, the region was a marshy jungle. Life proceeded in its usual fashion until a series of volcanic eruptions brought it to an end. Thick layers of ash that gave the Badlands their whitish color fell over the land.

If the Badlands not only betray the Earth's history through their amazing fossil fields, the land itself serves as a symbolic representation of the reckless and blind power that went into transforming Indian land into the United States.

It was here in the South Unit, at a place called Stronghold Table, that the Native American prophet named Wovoka held his Ghost Dances.

The Ghost Dance, which would last for days at a time, reinvigorated the people and renewed their crushed spirits. Yet it so threatened non-Natives that the U.S. Cavalry moved in to stop these spiritual gatherings, culminating in the 1890 bloody massacre of Wounded Knee, when more than two hundred unarmed men, women, and children were arrested for Ghost Dancing. Later, imprisoned in a church, they were surrounded, slaughtered, then buried in a mass grave. Among those murdered was the great chief Sitting Bull. The Ghost Dance religion died with them.

Empowered by the spirits of the Ghost Dancers and the restless Earth herself, those who participate today in spiritual quests in the Badlands say it is a fierce energy that permeates the land.

The Badlands are still ferocious yet full of wonder. The park covers 244,000 acres, and temperatures may range from -30° in the winter to 110° in the summer. The weather is known to change with awesome rapidity, transforming in a matter of minutes from sunny skies to lightning storms, high winds, and hail. Visiting in the spring or fall is advisable. The backcountry of the Badlands has no roads, only trails marked by the tread of bison. Unless you're a wilderness veteran, it is a good idea to spend time studying your park brochure. It will remind you to respect the animals, in particular the suspicious bison and the surprising rattlesnake. If you are a rock hound, tip the rock over with a long stick first. Underneath might be some rattler's favorite sleeping spot. Other than that, they will probably leave you alone.

Badlands National Park is situated in southern South Dakota and is open year round. It is divided into two areas. The North Unit starts at the Cedar Pass Visitor Center and the Cedar Pass Lodge, which is the best entry point. Well-marked trails lead from here to some of the fossil beds, scenic views, and the Sage Creek Wilderness Area for

Pawnee Ghost Dancer shirt with sacred icons.

camping. The South Unit, which is part of the Pine Ridge Indian Reservation, was incorporated into the park in 1976 and is administered by the park service in cooperation with the Sioux. This area features the White River Visitor Center. It does not have trails or campgrounds. To reach the Badlands, take Exit 110 or 131 off Interstate 90. Both of these exits lead to Route 240, which travels into the North Unit of the park. The South Unit's White River Visitor Center is on Route 27, traveling south from Route 44 at Scenic or north from Sharps Corner. For more information, write to or call Badlands National Park, PO Box 6, Interior, SD 57750; (605) 433-5361.

The Black Hills, South Dakota and Wyoming

The Black Hills of South Dakota, like the Badlands, are charged with the interwoven history of Native America, the Wild West, and the gold rush days. This is the land of Red Cloud and Wild Bill Hickok, Sitting Bull and Calamity Jane, Crazy Horse and General Custer. Its rich history looms large in much of American culture, in our music, folklore, and films.

The land itself is as dramatic as the legends it has spawned. The Black Hills feature tremendous forests with sacred mountains and timberland, stark fields, waterfalls, fossil beds, and scores of gem and mineral caves. Jewel Cave in the Black Hills is the fourth largest cave in the world and has sixty-nine miles of explored passageways that wind deep into the Earth. Scientists estimate that there are still hundreds of miles of Jewel Cave yet to be discovered and explored. Wind Cave, also in the area, is the eighth largest in the world. Of the seventy-two calcite crystal caves that are known to exist worldwide, sixty-eight of them are in the Black Hills. For rock hunters and spelunkers, this may be heaven on Earth.

For more information about the **Black Hills**, write to or call the South Dakota Department of Tourism, Capital Lake Plaza, Pierre, SD 57501; 1-800-843-1930.

The following three sites in the Black Hills are, in particular, places of tremendous spiritual significance.

Bear Butte, South Dakota

Nestled within the Black Hills is a haunting, strangely shaped mountain that for as long as the rivers have flowed and the flowers have bloomed has been revered by the Cheyenne and Sioux Indians. That mountain is called Bear Butte.

Rising fourteen hundred feet from the plains, its unusual form reminds many of a gargantuan sleeping bear. The Sioux call it Sleeping Bear Mountain or Mato Pah.

The bear is an important and omnipresent symbol in most Native American religions. Large and vital, sometimes vicious and ferocious, the bear, as we all know, retreats from the world during winter to hibernate. Because of its long sleeps, it came to be known to many Native Americans as the keeper of dreams.

For the Cheyenne, Bear Butte was where their great shaman, Sweet Medicine, received the four sacred arrows from the Great Spirit that formed the basis of the Cheyenne religion. These four arrows, symbolic of the four taboos, speak against murder, theft, adultery, and incest. True to the sacred number four, Sweet Medicine spent four years on the mountain before receiving his holy summons.

Bear Butte has been a holy shrine for centuries. Artifacts found there date back an incredible ten thousand years. The trails leading to the top of Bear Butte appear to be even older than that. A mere hundred years ago, Bear Butte served as a landmark for settlers and gold rush adventurers. But even today it remains mystical and serene, unswayed from its original purpose as a holy place. Bear Butte is still the keeper of dreams.

The Cheyenne, Sioux, Arapaho, and other Native Americans still gather at Bear Butte for sweat lodges, Sun Dances, and other spiritual ceremonies and vision quests, which is a testimony to Mato Pah's enduring power.

Bear Butte State Park can be reached by taking Interstate 90 from Sturgis and going east on route 34 for about 4 miles, then north on Route 79 for another 3 miles. The park covers 1,935 acres and has a visitor center that is open from May to September. The park and campgrounds are open year-round. For more information, write to or call Bear Butte State Park, Box 688, Sturgis, SD 57785; (605) 347-5240.

Crazy Horse Monument, South Dakota

Crazy Horse Monument is not a sacred site in the traditional sense of an ages-old holy mountain or a gathering place for native peoples. It is, however, a sacred site in the making, its spirit further empowered with each passing day as a gift to the present and future. It is an epic monument to Native Americans that is now being carved and blasted out of a mountain in the Black Hills. Once completed, Crazy Horse will stand 563 feet high and 641 feet long.

Imagine driving through the Black Hills. You turn a bend, pull over, and step out of your car to gape in wonder at the largest sculpture in the world. Taller than the Washington Monument, more massive than Egypt's Pyramid of Giza, it has been sculpted out of an entire granite mountain. Crazy Horse Monument, a memorial to Native Americans, looms in the distance.

It is as beautiful as it is staggering. Chief Crazy Horse, fierce and strong, is riding his rearing horse. His long hair flails in the wind down his back. His handsome features are grim and determined. He points straight ahead to the east. Underneath him are carved the words "My lands are where my dead lie buried." He and his horse appear to rush forward into the sky from the granite base.

Why Crazy Horse? You might ask. The choice is not hard to understand. Crazy Horse was a great chief and warrior of the Sioux Nation. He lived his life with unerring dignity and clearheaded faith in his people and their ways. Known to most Americans as the conqueror of General George Custer's army at the battle of Little Big Horn, Crazy Horse never surrendered or signed a treaty. Nor would he set foot on reservation land. He died through an act of treachery in 1877. Guaranteed safe conduct into a cavalry fort for negotiating purposes, Crazy Horse turned to leave when he sensed a trap. Sure enough, at that moment he was shot and stabbed by cavalry soldiers.

The story of how the sculpture came into being is as epic as the monument itself. In 1939, Chief Henry Standing Bear of the Sioux approached the young sculptor Korzcak Ziolkowski and asked if he might be willing to create a memorial to Native Americans. The awesome Mt. Rushmore "Shrine to Democracy" was just being completed in the Sioux's own precious Black Hills, and one can only imagine how they felt about it. Above all, they wanted to do something to let the white man know that Indians had great heroes as well.

The Sioux chose their artist well. Korzcak (as he preferred to be called) was a man of warrior spirit and tough-minded determination, a terrific match for his subject. Born in Boston, Korzcak was a self-taught artist and engineer who had just won first prize for his sculpture work at the 1939 New York World's Fair. Korzcak didn't merely consent to design the monument. He took to the task passionately and made it his responsibility to create an enduring and worthy memorial to Native Americans. A lesser man would have faltered.

With the design completed, the mountain chosen and secured, and some start-up funds finally raised, Crazy Horse was dedicated on June 3, 1948. Korzcak was forty when he began cutting down and shaping Thunderhead Mountain, the site chosen by Korzcak and Chief Henry Standing Bear's nephew.

He had for a time assisted Gutzon Borglum, the sculptor of Mt. Rushmore. Nevertheless, he tested and invented techniques as he went along, using heavy equipment and a lot of dynamite. He initially lived at the base of the mountain in a tent with virtually no money, but an iron will and his vision. Nothing stopped him. Whatever the obstacles, however, it was Korzcak's family, his wife and children, who helped the dream progress. Over the thirty-four years that Korzcak worked on Crazy Horse, he and his family moved over eight million tons of granite. Since his death in 1982, his family has continued the work according to detailed plans left by him. Korzcak knew Crazy Horse would require more than one lifetime.

Like the great chief himself, Korzcak is an inspiration. "By carving Crazy Horse," he said, "if I can give back to the Indian some of his pride and create the means to keep alive his culture and heritage, my life will have been worthwhile. . . . The world asks you one question: did you do your job? The answer is not 'I would have done it if people had been nicer . . . if I'd had the money . . . if I hadn't died.' Ifs don't count. The answer must be 'Yes!' "

The Crazy Horse complex features the Indian Museum of North America, which represents eighty tribes, Korzcak's studio and workshop, and a sixteen-foot-high scale model of the completed statue. Work-in-progress on the mountain, which is a mile from the visitor center, can be observed.

Crazy Horse model and Ziolkowski family in front of Crazy Horse Mountain

The nonprofit humanitarian project has had three goals: the completion of the memorial, the establishment of the Indian Museum of North America, and the development of the North American Indian University and Medical Training Center.

To reach **Crazy Horse Monument**, take U.S. 16, southwest from Rapid City or Interstate 90. Travel 36 miles. It is 16 miles from Mt. Rushmore on U.S. 16-385. It is open year-round. Crazy Horse is financed only by a small per-car admission fee and donations by the public. If you're not planning a trip to South Dakota anytime soon and would like to be part of this sacred site in the making, you can send a donation. For hours or more information, write to or call Crazy Horse Monument, Avenue of the Chiefs, Crazy Horse, SD 57730-9998; (605) 673-4681.

Devil's Tower National Monument, Wyoming

Devil's Tower is the stuff from which myths and legends are made. It's a bold, unearthly-looking rock tower with large crevices down its sides. It seemingly defies explanation as it rises from the surrounding land as high as a hundred-story building. There's nothing else quite like it.

Native Americans called Devil's Tower Mato Tipila, or Bear Lodge. This Sioux legend about the discovery of Mato Tipila was told by Short Bull in 1932 and recorded by Dick Stone and Shirley Rathbun in the book *First Encounters: Indian Legends of Devil's Tower*:

> In the Sioux Tribe, long ago, was a brave warrior who often went alone into the wilderness where he would fast and worship the Great Spirit in solitude. Being alone helped him to strengthen his courage so that in the future he could carry out his plans.
>
> One day this warrior took his buffalo skull and went alone into the wilderness to worship. Standing at the base of Mato Tipila, after he had worshiped for two days, he suddenly found himself on top of this high rock. He was very much frightened as he did not know how he would get down. After appealing to the Great Spirit, he went to sleep. When he

Wyoming Travel Commission

Devil's Tower

awoke he was very glad to find that he was again at the base of this high rock.

He saw that he was standing at the door of a big bear's lodge. There were footprints of a very big bear. He could tell that the cracks in the big rock were made by the big bear's claws. So he knew that all the time he had been on top of the big rock, he had been standing on a big bear's lodge.

From this time on his nation called this big high rock Mato Tipila. They went there often to worship. The Buffalo Skull is still on top of this big rock and can be seen on the highest point.

In many Native American legends about the tower's formation, people are being chased by a giant bear and pray to the Great Spirit to save them. Under their feet, pushing them upward toward the sky, rises a tremendous rock. The giant bear is so angry he claws at the side of the growing mountain, and these are the crevices that are still there today. Often the spirits of those saved are not abandoned on top of the tower, but transformed into star groups such as the Pleiades or the Big Dipper.

Though a number of tribes called the Black Hills home and had their individual territories, Mato Tipila was shared as a sacred area for worship and vision quest by the honored members of all tribes and warriors. Sometimes chiefs and elders of the Sioux were buried near the tower.

When the name was changed to Devil's Tower in 1875 by a treaty-breaking scientific team that was there to confirm reports of gold, the Indians thought it was pretty silly. If there was a devil in the tower, they pointed out, they wouldn't have been going there for hundreds of years to worship God. But by 1875, they had realized the white man had a very different relationship to the land than they did.

Similar to the pervasive attraction of many sacred sites from culture to culture, the tower later became a natural gathering place of ranchers and relatives in Wyoming who would meet there for July 4th celebrations. In 1906, President Teddy Roosevelt made Devil's Tower the first of eighteen national monuments to be protected under the new Antiquities Act.

It has even played a role in contemporary culture. Devil's Tower was the serendipitous location Steven Spielberg used for the starship landing in his film *Close Encounters of the Third Kind*. No doubt, a very logical choice. With centuries of worship to the Great Spirit and vision quest played out at Devil's Tower, it has probably been and still is the site of all sorts of encounters.

Devil's Tower is 1,267 feet high, and climbing it is a challenge that attracts several thousand people a year. The first recorded climb was on July 4, 1893, when William Rodgers and Willard Ripley scaled the tower, and the event was a big celebration. Their wives ran the refreshment stand down below and sold bits of the American flag raised on the summit as souvenirs. At present, there are over a hundred climbing routes on the tower, most of which go to the summit.

Devil's Tower National Monument, in the northeast corner of Wyoming, which is also considered part of the Black Hills, is reached by taking Route 14 northwest of Sundance, Wyoming, for 28 miles. Open year-round, campground available. For more information, write to or call Superintendent, Devil's Tower National Monument, Devil's Tower, WY 82714; (307) 467-5370.

The Bighorn Medicine Wheel, Wyoming

All over the center of the North American continent, from the Mississippi River to the Rockies, from Canada to Texas, the plains are spotted with thousands of circular stone medicine wheels left by the Native Americans who lived and roamed there. Enduring time and weather, the rings, some of which are more than five thousand years old, were once all assumed to be, and thus labeled, *tipi rings.*

True, stones were used to hold down the edges of a tipi and left in place when the tribe moved on. But other rings, too large to be dismissed as mere tipi rings, were until recently thought to have been created for council gatherings and worship, and most of them probably were constructed for that purpose.

One previously unrecognized factor, however, is now receiving a lot of attention and changing how we look at the medicine wheels. Many of them, like Stonehenge, Woodhenge at Cahokia (see Chapter 4), Calendar One in Vermont (see Chapter 3), and other pre-Columbian ruins, were carefully designed to align with and reflect the movements of certain stars and planets. One purpose, perhaps the primary function, seems to have been the prediction of seasonal changes. Whatever else the shamans and medicine men looked for in the stars or in the daylight as the sun and moon rose is as yet unknown.

A true cosmic puzzle, the meaning of the medicine wheel is just beginning to unravel. Seasons or not, alignments or not, medicine wheels are known to Native Americans as

Wyoming Travel Commission

Bighorn Medicine Wheel

very sacred places, interpreted by astronomer-priests. Surely only the most spiritually and scientifically gifted of the tribe gathered at the medicine wheels. There, based on their magic and observations, they could interpret the starry dances of the Sun God, the constellations, various star groups, and other celestial friends. In their interpretations lay the fate of the community for one more year.

The astronomer-priest, as much as the military leader of the tribe, was the most important person among many ancient peoples. One cannot help wondering if today's new class of intrepid archaeoastronomers, pursuing their painstaking work of measuring and surveying ancient sites for their sky connections, are merely doing so again, maybe the second or third time around, recovering rather than discovering past knowledge.

Laid out with large rocks, medicine wheels usually have stone spokes extending from a central rock pile, or cairn.

The central cairn, with its outwardly radiating spokes, may be seen as reflecting the sun and its rays. It can also be interpreted as a symbol of motion.

Medicine wheels were usually built at high altitudes, on mountaintops or in elevated valleys. At just what point the practice originated is unknown. And there are other mysteries.

Why would an immobile calendar saluting the annual solar solstices, so integral to agricultural societies, be built by nomadic tribes? Many wheels are located in the Rocky Mountains and isolated areas of the Southwest, in unfertile lands. It must have been an arduous trip, a pilgrimage, just to reach them. The medicine wheels may have been built only to declare the time of the sacred Sun Dance. Or, they may be about something not yet imagined. Surely the sky-gazers were watching for more than the sun. Something out there was very holy indeed.

The Big Horn Medicine Wheel is a stone circle about ninety feet in diameter surrounding a central cairn twelve feet in diameter and two feet high. From the cairn radiate twenty-eight spokes. Six other cairns are spaced on the outside of the rim.

John Eddy, solar physicist and archaeoastronomer, is an important unraveler of the Big Horn Medicine Wheel. With his family, he traveled to Big Horn in 1971 for *National Geographic* and carefully recorded one of the wheel's central secrets:

> In darkness the next morning we trudged up the snowy slope. We trudged up the cold trail in boots still wet from the day before. Three hours later, as a pink sky slowly brightened, we crouched nearly frozen behind the lonely outer cairn and awaited the coming sunrise. The direction of the first glow told us we could not be far wrong. And then, in majestic quiet, the great red ball of the sun appeared, exactly in line with the cairns. In the biting cold we felt happily warm. For all the summers since the wheel was built, sunrise had moved along the horizon to perform this striking solar spectacle—with no one there to watch.

As Eddy and his family discovered, the stone points of the circle line up exactly with the rising and setting sun of the summer solstice. And there is more. Eddy showed that other stones in the circle also line up with the three brightest stars of the early morning hours of summer: Aldebaran in the constellation Taurus, Rigel in Orion, and Sirius in Canis Major. In the summer, these stars can be seen right before the sun rises, before they quickly fade into daylight. Astronomers call this phenomenon rising heliacally.

Another enigma envelops the number twenty-eight. There are twenty-eight spokes in the wheel. Most obviously, the lunar cycle is twenty-eight days, and many Native Americans told time by moons. The star Rigel also rises heliacally twenty-eight days after Aldebaran, and Sirius does the same twenty-eight days after Rigel.

John Eddy's investigation showed that the spokes may have been a later addition. It appears that the medicine wheel is at least two hundred years old and may be up to seven hundred. If the spokes were a later addition to the wheel, it only serves to prove its value over time, a part of the religious worship of the people in the area for centuries.

While the parade of U.S. history rolled relentlessly on, the Big Horn Medicine Wheel remained unknown to the white man for several hundred years. Tucked away on a level ridge near the apex of a 10,000-foot-high mountain in the Bighorn range, it is protected by deep snows most of the year.

Though it was known by the different native tribes that hunted in the area, and possibly even used by them for ceremonies, it was left undisturbed. Then, when the rush for gold brought prospectors and settlers to the Rocky Mountains a little over a hundred years ago, it came to the attention of the white man. They found it and fortunately left it alone. Later it became known as the medicine wheel, *medicine* meaning supernatural power in Native American religion.

About seventy years ago, archaeologists began to investigate it. They queried the local tribes about who built the medicine wheel. Many received blank stares and answers of "It was here when we came." But other responses were as vague and steeped in lore as the Chocktaw's tales of the Mound Builders.

Shoshone legends told of the construction of the medicine wheel by a race of "little people." The legend lends itself to theories of an E.T. colony. Or perhaps they were second-race men, that Lilliputianlike breed of *Homo sapiens* that figures in folklore throughout the world.

The Shoshone legend speaks of a horde of tiny men in the Wyoming area that attacked a hunting party with stones. Though the tale stops there, the mystery doesn't. In 1932, two gold prospectors dynamited a stone gulch in Wyoming that opened up a cave. Inside the cave sat a mummified fourteen-inch-high man. Later x-rayed and studied by scientists at Harvard University, the American Museum of Natural History, and the Boston Museum, the creature was concluded to have been a human-like anthropoid, full-grown when he or she died. They were unable to say how long ago the creature lived.

The Big Horn Medicine Wheel is ninety-six hundred feet up Medicine Mountain in the Bighorn National Forest. Medicine Mountain is 27 miles east of Lovell in northcentral Wyoming. Route 14A cuts through the forest and will take you almost all the way to the wheel. In case of a summer snowstorm, you may have to park about 2 miles away and trek the rest of the distance. Because the Medicine Wheel may be inaccessible most of the year due to snowstorms, the best bet is June, July, or August. If you do visit in June, be sure to witness the risings of the three bright stars Aldebaran, Rigel, and Sirius as they usher in solstice sunrise on June 21. For more information, write to or call the forest rangers' office, PO Box 367, Lovell, WY 82431; (307) 548-6541.

Moose Mountain Medicine Wheel, Saskatchewan

The medicine wheel on top of Moose Mountain in southern Saskatchewan, Canada, may be at least a thousand years older than the Bighorn. As documented by Dr. Eddy and archaeologists Alice and Tom Kehoe, Moose Mountain's five cairns appear, incredibly enough, to have the same alignments and pattern as the Bighorn even though they are over four hundred miles apart. The cairns align precisely with the solstice sunrise and sunset and the risings of Aldebaran, Rigel, and Sirius. "Matched like fingerprints," John Eddy has said. Most likely they were part of the same religious tradition that stretched across the region for millennia.

There are quite a number of medicine wheels in Alberta and Saskatchewan. Unlike the Bighorn, which has a sign and a road leading to it, the Canadian wheels are located on private lands or tucked away on the hillsides. Unfortunately, many of them are not in the state or natural park system. For more information on how to get to Moose Mountain and others, write to or call the Archeological Survey of Alberta, 8820 112th St., Edmonton, AB T6G 2PB, Canada; (403) 427-2355; or in Saskatchewan, Curator, Archeology Department, Museum of Natural History, Wascana Park, Regina, Saskatchewan S4P 3V7, Canada; (306) 787-2815

Making Your Own Medicine Wheel

It is said that the line that creates a circle never ends, just as the circle of life never ends. The circle represents eternity. This is why it is a sacred symbol common to so many different cultures.

The medicine wheel is also, of course, a circle. It pays homage to the four directions and is meant in part to give the celebrant a sense of where he or she is in the physical universe. From inside a medicine wheel, we can check the sky for solar and lunar equinoxes, as well as the positions of various star groups, and feel a sense of locality on the earth.

At these sacred places, ancient forefathers celebrated through their rituals where they were, how they were, and what they were. Parts of the medicine wheel represent all these things. Above all, the wheels are places where people gathered, humbled themselves, and worshiped the universe and life itself.

It is quite easy to make your own medicine wheel. One must approach the process, however, with the utmost sincerity. An earnest willingness to get to know yourself and connect with a sacred site is what is most important.

Create the four directions in this order: south, north, west, and finally east. If you were to draw south at the bottom of a page of paper, then north, and so on in that order, you would see the number 4 appear. Four is a very sacred number to Native Americans because it represents the four directions.

These four directions represent aspects of ourselves. South, the first stop on the medicine wheel, symbolizes our raw self, our feelings, emotions, and gut reactions. It is also where the emotional element water resides. The north represents wisdom and intellect, the rational mind. West signifies death of form and matter and its transformation. Every organic form in the universe must die. This includes everything from stars and planets to animals and plants to you and me. So when you turn to the west in a medicine wheel, that is what you must contemplate. In the east is that which does not die. The east symbolizes the spirit, life eternal, evolution, and illumination. It is the goal of the medicine wheel. We humans are composed of all of these elements.

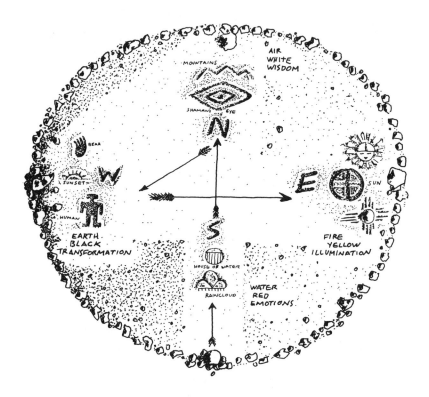

Making Your Own Medicine Wheel.

With compass in hand, you can take these concepts and connect with a sacred site. Always move clockwise.

Start with the south. Face in that direction and make a small offering if you like. Native Americans used raw tobacco, for example. Then ask, Who am I? Plumb the depths of your emotions. You already know the answer, although at first you may think you do not. Once you have your answer, give sincere thanks to the Spirit of the South.

Turn to the north. Ask, Why am I here? For what purpose have I been given this life? What is my goal? After you are clear about the answer, give sincere thanks to the Spirit of the North.

Moving clockwise, face west. Think of the day that dies in the west. As west represents death, contemplate what it is that must die inside of you in order for you to reach your goal. It might be a vice or a particular attitude. What is it? Once you know, give sincere thanks to the Spirit of the West.

Finally, turn to the east. You're on your way home. Meditate on what you've learned. Once you're focused on exactly what that is, you've reached illumination. You've become part of the medicine wheel. Give thanks for the knowledge you have received.

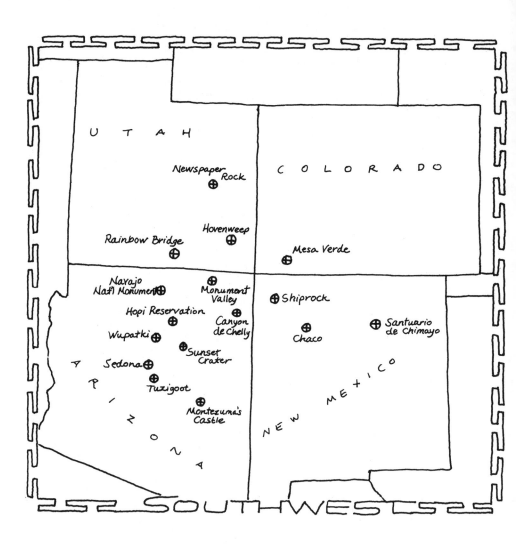

7
THE STUNNING
SOUTHWEST

The American Southwest is filled with tales of magic and death, color and spirit. Its volatile and unique topography comprises a profound and austere beauty—a beauty underlined, however, with the threat of danger. It is the rattlesnake beneath the pink quartz slab or the flash flood that sweeps into a canyon from nowhere. It is the deadly heat of the summer midday sun or the strange encounter with the wise loner who lives out there somewhere, who just as easily could have been part of a dream. It is the land of the empty canteen and the sign that declares, "Next town 95 miles." Cliché or not, the sign speaks the truth. Outside the cities and towns, life is not easy here.

Captured in Georgia O'Keeffe's vivid, metaphysical paintings, this is the magic land that fills the imagination and challenges the soul, where reality may tilt on its axis to your benefit or chagrin, where you can revel or crumble in its power. Strange things happen in the Southwest. The region is famous for them.

The Southwest has a seductive quality that keeps those who visit returning again and again. People who have tapped into the magic of the Southwest sometimes lose interest in other parts of the world. They become heady with it, and their talk becomes littered with their aspirations to buy "a piece of land in the desert." Like all land across the planet, each place speaks to us in a different way with different energy, sometimes attracting or alternately repelling us. The Southwest most poignantly does both, and it is hard to forget the feeling once you have been there.

To the urbanized eye, much of the land seems barren. Yet this is another of its illusions. It is alive on every level— animal, plant, and mineral, physical and metaphysical. Photographers are eternally struggling to capture the shades and shadows of its rocks and canyons that are so imbued with spirit.

Spiritually, the Southwest is empowered with the triumph and tragedy of some of Native America's most gifted peoples, such as the Hopi, Navajo, Zuni, and many others, as well as their mysterious ancestors. The land is spotted with traces of these advanced ancestral civilizations, which we know as the Hohokam, Mogollon, and Anasazi.

The remains of their once-flourishing cultures are everywhere: stone petroglyphs, trails winding in and out of the steepest canyons, multistoried apartment buildings tucked away in inaccessible cliffsides, ceremonial centers, astronomical watch stations, and ancient irrigation canals. All these provide us with the shards of southwestern history. In a different time, from the Rio Grande to the Rocky Mountains, when the Southwest was not so dry, the Anasazi and their brethren cultures, the Hohokam and Mogollon, prospered for more than ten centuries.

Spirit dwells not only in the soul but in the Earth itself. Sacred sites manifest this, whoever their keepers are. In the Southwest, this is demonstrated most keenly.

THE HOHOKAM AND MOGOLLON

Eerily similar to the Mound Builders east of the Mississippi, the great cultures of the Southwest began and died out at roughly the same times under equally unknown circumstances.

There is evidence that their early beginnings as a cohesive culture came around 500 B.C. and that their civilization built to its height from A.D. 500 to 1300. Although there is not much evidence pointing to trade between the southwestern and mound-building peoples, both appear to have had well-worn trade routes extending to the Rockies as evidenced by their use of obsidian. As well, both civilizations appear to have been heavily influenced through contact with the Mayans and the rest of MesoAmerica.

The Hohokam are thought to have migrated into what is present-day Arizona from Mexico and settled there in approximately 300 B.C. The word *Hohokam* comes from the Pima Indian word meaning "all used up," evidently in response to desert lands they inhabited. Nevertheless, they were highly skilled farmers, coaxing both spring and autumn crops from the land via a complicated and sophisticated irrigation system. In fact, to this day, some of Arizona's modern irrigation and waterworks are built over the ancient ones. Their communities are identified architecturally by adobe buildings, ball courts, and low platform mounds. Artifacts include rubber balls, red and white pottery often featuring rows of dancers holding hands, feminine figurines for Earth and goddess worship, shell jewelry from the Gulf of California, and gorgeous copper bells.

It is easy to imagine the sound of those bells as they chimed in the windows of an adobe building on a dry and windy night. Without a doubt, despite the long, hard labor of their days, the Hohokam loved music, dance, and beauty.

In the last several centuries before their end, they meshed with the mysterious Anasazi and another smaller culture, the Sinagua (from the Spanish, meaning "without water"). By the fifteenth century they were gone due to the usual speculative reasons of crop failures, raids, disease, natural disasters. The dry desert once transformed into fertile cropland returned to being the arid zone for which Arizona is named.

Named after the jagged ridges that comprise part of the Continental Divide, the Mogollon culture extended all the way through northern Mexico up through northcentral New

Mexico, overlapping with the lands of the Anasazi. With a much simpler lifestyle than their Hohokam and Anasazi neighbors, they nevertheless eked out a steady, consistent existence for about twelve centuries, until they blended with or were overwhelmed by the great Anasazi culture. Together they formed what is known as the Western Pueblo (*pueblo* is Spanish for "village").

Mogollon pottery was red and brown earthenware covered with spiral and zigzag designs. Like the Hohokam, the Mogollon's farming skills were prodigious. They farmed the high, dry hillsides by building stone terraces, engineering them to prevent erosion and to use every drop of runoff rainwater. In the center of their village was a Great Kiva, or circular ceremonial center. When the Mogollon and the more northern Anasazi become one culture about A.D. 1000, their population increased and their cities grew. Irrigation canals were constructed, and their artworks became more elaborate. In whatever ways the three cultures maintained their own identities, there was still much cross-fertilization among them. Still, it wouldn't be long before the ways of the great Anasazi dominated.

THE ANASAZI

With a name derived from the Navajo meaning "Ancient Ones," the Anasazi were a prehistoric people known for their famous stone masonry and adobe buildings done in three different styles, all of them known as *pueblo*. Some of these pueblos are so enduring they still house people today. Yet despite the decades of extensive excavations of Anasazi ruins, the true puzzle of their lives and the astronomy and worship that shaped them is only now being understood.

Anasazi lands covered most of the Four Corners region, extending through southern Utah and southwestern Colorado and covering the northern halves of Arizona and New Mexico. Their ruins consist of both small villages accommodating a few families to large cities with many multi-leveled buildings containing hundreds of rooms and huge ceremonial kivas. Despite the dry land, they cultivated enough corn, squash, and beans among other staples to provide for their growing population over many centuries.

Anasazi women cut their hair short, and the men wore it long. Their clothing consisted of soft, fine furs and woven fabric made of cotton from their fields. The men, or at least the single ones, lived in the kivas, which were also used as social centers. Sometimes the apartment areas were matrilineally oriented, being reserved for or given priority to women and children. The women comprised the stable family unit. If a woman wasn't pleased with her man, she would simply put his belongings outside the home. From there, he could go back to his mother's house or stay in areas provided for men with no houses to go to. Land was also passed down through daughters. The use of land, however, was more important than who owned it. If a family ceased to use the land, someone else could cultivate it.

Politically, the Anasazi seem to have had a system of share-and-share-alike under the guidance of their elders and priests. There is evidence that goods and necessities were gathered and redistributed accordingly. They traded with the Indians of the plains, California, and Mexico. Though influenced initially by the Mayans, they also eventually traded with the Aztecs and may have been, to some extent, dependent culturally and spiritually on the supercultures to the south.

Anasazi artifacts include delightful multicolored, multishaped pottery decorated with all types of animals and whimsical designs. Their luxurious turquoise jewelry was so richly designed it is imitated to this day. Their baskets were finely and intricately woven. Because much of their housing was protected by overhanging cliffs or was partially subterranean, some of their baskets and clothing have survived for some two thousand years. This also preserved a few of their dead, whose corpses simply dried up in their stone burial pits.

The Anasazi were dispersed by the fourteenth century. They may have started to abandon their towns some decades earlier. The catalyst for their demise is unknown but

Anasazi pottery.

possibly was a drought that swept the land for twenty-five years beginning around 1275. What is creepy is that many of the Anasazi left their belongings as though they would be back later that day. But they never returned.

Though they may not have matched some of the Mexican or other cultures on Earth at the time, they were not far behind in their development. In some ways, they were a much more humane and enlightened people than both their European and Mesoamerican counterparts. Unfortunately, there is no telling what more they could have accomplished had they continued to thrive. Again like the Mound Builders, they disbanded into smaller groups and transformed over the next several hundred years into contemporary tribes. There is, however, one major difference. Whereas many of the tribes in the East claimed no knowledge of the Mound Builders, the southwesterners retained a very strong sense of their forebears, the Ancient Ones.

Many of their religious traditions were passed down to

them by the Anasazi and quite possibly other cultures of antiquity that we know nothing about. It provided the wisdom by which they were able to survive and prosper in a land deemed cruel and unusual by later settlers.

So in conflict were the white men with the Southwest that it is possible they never would have bothered much with it at all, were it not for the precious metals found in her soil. Silver and greed allayed their fears and frustrations. When they had taken their fill in a matter of a few short years, they abandoned their villages, spawning a new kind of western ruin, the ghost town. Not surprisingly, the lust for uranium quickly brought them back.

We tend to speak of our relationship with Native Americans as a thing of the past. We talk about what has been done with no thought of what is happening today.

As the Indians watched their sacred lands become reservations, so they are still watching as what is left is compromised or whittled away by Congress, nuclear energy and other energy conglomerates, and developers. Most recently, Congress appropriated 160,000 acres belonging to the ancient and secluded Acoma tribe of southcentral New Mexico and gave it to the National Park Service. The Acoma fought desperately to retain a mere 40 acres of their most sacred grounds and were summarily refused. Thus the Cane of Peace given to them by Abraham Lincoln is tragically broken.

Still, one can visit many of the sacred grounds in the magical Southwest. But state lines, a late addition to the Southwest, are difficult to reconcile when it comes to the area's sacred sites. A site can be in one state and the address in another. To minimize confusion, we will travel counterclockwise from Colorado's Mesa Verde, through the Four Corners region, into Utah, down to Arizona, and into New Mexico.

New Mexico's nickname is Land of Enchantment. That sobriquet could apply to the entire Southwest, where both body and soul fare best with four-wheel drive.

Mesa Verde, Colorado

*"I looked up and saw, under an overhanging cliff,
a great cavernlike place in which was situated
what seemed like a small ruined city. In the
dusk and the silence, the great blue vault hung
over me like a mirage. The solemn grandeur
of the outlines was breathtaking."*
—Al Wetherill, amateur archaeologist

Al Wetherill, a southwestern rancher, wrote that in his autobiography about seeing one of Mesa Verde's ruins for the first time in the 1890s. What Wetherill had discovered was the Cliff Palace, the largest Anasazi cliff dwelling in America.

After Mesa Verde was abandoned by the Anasazi in the 1300s, it remained unknown to Anglos for five centuries. The Native Americans in the area who knew about it left it alone. With a few rare exceptions, they never even led or guided explorers to any of the ruins. It was up to the new Americans to stumble on them for themselves.

In 1874, it finally happened, when William Henry Jackson, a member of a U.S. Geological and Geographical Survey of the Territories party, happened on one of the ruins and photographed it. The photo was widely reprinted in the East and ignited considerable curiosity. But it would still be a few decades before the rediscovery of Mesa Verde would begin in earnest.

Richard and Al Wetherill were ranchers who lived in the surrounding Mancos Valley. For years they had been uncovering pottery fragments, arrow points, stone axes, and other artifacts they felt were clear evidence that the area had once been home to an immense population. Another indication of ancient inhabitants was the abundance of ruins of individual stone houses that were scattered throughout the Mancos Canyon and its tributaries.

Following the directions of a man who had wintered his cattle in Mancos Canyon, Al Wetherill made an exploratory trip into the overgrown canyon in 1882. After about ten or

Jack Olsen

Mesa Verde

twelve miles, he was about to turn back toward home when he sighted a minor cliff dwelling later named Sandal House. Although the importance of that find took a while to register, it was not that long afterward that the brothers launched their eighteen-year archaeological crusade.

In their book, *The Wetherills of the Mesa Verde*, the brothers describe how they probed the back canyons that everyone else considered worthless. The Ute Indian trails in these areas, if present at all, were quite overgrown. The stunted-growth trees and brush could easily wear out the toughest man. It was on one of his exploratory outings that Al saw the Cliff Palace, which was later named by his brother, Richard.

It was stunning to see and impossible to reach. It was left for his brother, Richard, and another rancher, Charles Mason, to find a more accessible mesatop route into the village. Unlike many of the ruins they previously had explored and excavated, the Cliff Palace had not been plundered. Similar to those who opened the doors to the tombs of the pyramids, seeing the ruin so completely untouched chilled them.

> Things were arranged in the rooms as if the people might just have been out visiting somewhere. Perfect specimens of pottery sat on the floors and other convenient locations; stone implements and household equipment were where the housewives had last used the articles; evidence of children playing house even as children do now; estufas where the men congregated, leaving the ancient ashes of altar fires long dead. There was no indication of violence toward the people themselves. . . . We could almost see them around us. We could watch them at work in the fields, with the dogs barking and the turkeys calling; the men coming in from work; women busy at their looms or grinding corn for the midday meal; the children playing near. . . . It was so much like treading "holy ground" to go into those peaceful-looking homes of a vanished people.

Mason and the Wetherills began a campaign to let the world know of their astonishing finds. Although they were met with indifference throughout Colorado, word spread quickly to more appreciative ears.

In 1891, archaeology buff Baron Gustav Nordenskjold of Sweden did the first systematic excavations at Mesa Verde. Yet, upon leaving, he boxed up dozens upon dozens of artifacts to take with him. The local people tried to stop his plundering, but there was no law to support their objections. The looting was continued by the baron and others until the federal Antiquities Act was passed in 1906. That act founded the Mesa Verde National Park and prohibited the removal of ancient artifacts. After many years, the baron's great collection of Mesa Verde artifacts ended up in Helsinki, where it is housed to this day in Finland's National Museum.

Mesa Verde (Spanish for "green table") was the first national park dedicated to the preservation of the works of man. Created by President Theodore Roosevelt in 1906, its 52,000 acres are estimated to contain over 5,000 Anasazi ruins. More than twenty major sites have been excavated and stabilized and are open to the public. Fortunately, there are still sites that have been left untouched for future generations.

The history and architecture of Mesa Verde represent the rise of the Anasazi culture in the Southwest. Though many of their villages and those of the Sinaguan culture were separated by several hundred miles, they all confoundingly followed the same leaps in development at the same times. Isolated from one another as their communities were, there had to have been much communication between them. As it would happen, they evolved, prospered, and dissolved away as a single entity.

The first Anasazi settled in the area around A.D. 550. These once nomadic people began planting the mesatops with corn, beans, and squash to supplement the gathering of wild plants and the hunting of deer, rabbits, squirrels, and other game. For the next couple of hundred years, the Anasazi did not live in the cliff dwellings so famous today— that would happen centuries later—but rather in small villages built on top of the mesas.

These early villages consisted of clusters of pithouses dug a few feet into the ground to take advatage of natural cooling. The Anasazi were brilliant at taking advantage of the elements for natural cooling as well as passive solar heating, constructing their houses in harmony with the environment. A pithouse typically contained a squarish living room, four corner timbers to support the roof, an air deflector, and a storage antechamber. Also featured was a hole in the floor known as a sipapu, symbolic entrance to the underworld. Many southwestern tribes believe they came into this world from a lower one, underground. The origins for this belief could well go back to the Anasazi, for whom spirit touched every aspect of their lives.

Around A.D. 750, the Anasazi of Mesa Verde began build-ing their houses above ground, with upright walls made of poles and adobe mud. By A.D. 1000, their construction skills had advanced to a precise and supple use of stone masonry.

Using only sharp-edged chert, a flintlike rock, craftsmen were able to cut uniformly straight, rectangular blocks about the size of a loaf of bread out of sandstone. These blocks were then transported by the thousands, along with giant roof-supporting timbers, to construction sites without benefit of the wheel. However, the wheel would not have been much help in transporting the blocks up and down the cliffsides. It would be interesting to know what crane devices they used. The blocks were then fashioned to fit corners and curved walls and placed in straight courses with an astonishing exactness. The mortar between the blocks was a mix of mud and water.

By 1100, considered to be the beginning of Mesa Verde's "classic period," round and square towers began to be incorporated into the architecture. Dwelling walls often rose two or three stories high and were joined into units of fifty rooms or more. The pithouse evolved into the kiva and served a function similar to our churches. An extensive water system constructed to serve the populace included a man-made reservoir (known today as Mummy Lake) ninety feet in diameter and twelve feet deep, a canal that diverted water to the reservoir, and a crop irrigation network. Pottery, weaving, jewelry, and tool-making also flourished.

Then, about 1200, the Anasazi of Mesa Verde began moving out of their mesatop pueblos and into alcoves and caves underneath the cliffs. What caused this move we don't know. It may have been a defense against invaders or a suddenly even harsher environment. Most of the cliff dwellings extant today were built in the middle decades of the 1200s. Architecturally, there is no standard ground plan. The builders customized each structure to its space. Inside, many rooms were plastered and decorated with painted designs. Highly social beings, the Anasazi lived in closely with each other, and much of their daily life took place in the open courtyards in front of their apartments.

The Anasazi occupied their magnificent cliff houses for less than a hundred years. By A.D. 1300, Mesa Verde was deserted. Scientists have documented a twenty-three-year drought that struck the area at the end of the thirteenth century that is the most likely reason the culture fell apart. Otherwise, we are left with the same questions and suppositions about their demise that plague the study of many ancient peoples: Did disease wipe them out? Did armed invaders destroy them? Was the land depleted? Was it simply a drought? The answer may be found in the future, but for now there is none.

Mesa Verde has five cliff dwellings visitors can enter during the summer months. During the winter, only one can be explored safely. Two sites at Mesa Verde are especially fascinating.

The Cliff Palace

A ten-minute drive from the excellent Mesa Verde museum, the Cliff Palace is built into an alcove 325 feet long and 90 feet deep. During summer months, visitors can take a quarter-mile self-guided walking tour that requires climbing four ten-foot ladders. The Cliff Palace was not a palace to the Anasazi, for they did not have royalty. It was, rather, a large apartment complex that housed a population estimated to have been between 200 and 250 people. It contains 23 ceremonial kivas and 220 rooms. The rectangular tower rises to almost four stories in height and is a masterpiece of construction. In its third-story room is a beautiful red and white wall painting that has withstood the onslaught of more than six centuries.

The Sun Temple

Directly across from the Cliff Palace, on the point of a fingerlike mesa formed by Cliff and Fewkes canyons, is the haunting Sun Temple. This Anasazi construction is completely unlike any other. It is a surface site and not a cliff

Natural sun symbol, Mesa Verde.

dwelling, and its ground plan is shaped in the form of a giant D. Even though little of the original edifice remains, it appears to have been built in two sections. The Sun Temple probably served a religious function of rites and rituals. There is one feature of the temple in particular that has engendered considerable debate as to its purpose. It is known as the Sun Shrine.

Found in the southwestern corner of the temple, the Sun Shrine is a peculiar symbol enclosed on three sides, on the east by the wall of the Sun Temple and on the north and south by two short walls built at right angles to the main building wall. The symbol itself, which looks like a large sunflower, is wrought in sandstone. It is less than two feet in diameter and is composed of two parts—a central well or basin from one to six inches deep and a border of radial ridges and furrows surrounding the bowl. This sunflower-like symbol of the sun appears over and over again in pueblo ruins across the Southwest in rock art and artifacts. But this one is very different.

After painstaking examination, geologists have declared the sun symbol the product of natural sandstone erosion, not of carving. There is little doubt, however, that the Anasazi cut it out of its natural sandstone location, transported it to the Sun Temple, and built it into what appears to have been an altar or shrine.

Mesa Verde National Park is located in southwestern Colorado. The park entrance is midway between the towns of Cortez and Mancos, off U.S. 160. It is a 21-mile drive from the entrance to the park headquarters. The park is open year round during daylight hours. Morfield Campground is 4 miles from the park entrance and is open from approximately May to mid-October. There is one motel on the grounds of the park, and numerous other lodging facilities are in nearby Mancos, Cortez, Dolores, and Durango. A picnic area is located near the museum on Chapin Mesa and is open year-round. Altitudes in the park vary from 6,000 to 8,500 feet. Cliff dwellings may be entered only when accompanied by a ranger. For more information, write to or call Mesa Verde National Park, CO 81330; (303) 529-4465.

The Canyonlands, Utah

The entire Canyonlands area of southeastern Utah is provocative and dramatic. Though generally less publicized and with less of a film and television history than, say, the Grand Canyon or Monument Valley, the Utah canyons are nevertheless enthralling. For those who have spent a lot of time exploring and camping in the mountains of Colorado, California, or other areas in the West, a week or more in Utah's high country may be an astonishing discovery.

As natural sites, the Utah Canyonlands may not be Earth's largest canyons, with the tallest waterfalls or deepest gorges, yet they share an extreme and exquisite quality. They are extreme in color, temperature, texture, and shape. They are also extreme in history. Their crags and gullies have securely hidden people for thousands of years, from Paleo-Indians to the Anasazi, the Utes and Paiute Indians, the Navajo fleeing from Kit Carson, and quite a number of Old West fugitives from the law. Go to Moab and take a walk with Butch Cassidy. The Canyonlands were where anyone and anything could lose themselves. As Mormon settler

Ebeneezer Bryce had to say about his namesake, Bryce Canyon, "It's one helluva place to lose a cow."

Representative of the extreme nature of the canyons is the story behind Dead Horse Point, which is now a state park. Cowboys used the mesa point to corral wild mustangs. Having gathered up a rather large number of them, they captured the ones they wanted and fenced off the rest, where they died of thirst two thousand feet above the Colorado River, which flowed on three sides of the point.

In Canyonlands National Park (which is only one of many parks in the region), there is a macabre thirty-square-mile area called the Maze. Featuring one twisting, curving bend or eroded rock canyon after another, the Maze is something even the most prolific fantasy artist could not design. One U.S. captain who was exploring the area in the 1850s called it worthless and impractical. And he didn't even get to the Maze.

Certainly not all the history is this harsh, but spiritually it is this poignant. The land isn't particularly suited for humans. With their attunement to the Earth, the Anasazi and a few later Indian tribes successfully made the area their home. However, whites did not settle there until the late nineteenth century. Today it is still not for the pampered, and those with a fear of heights will never make it up some of those spine-tingling cliffside roads—or down them either. It is land designed for Jeeps, horses, backpacking, and boats. There are many comfortable and luxurious lodges and well-paved scenic drives, but at some point you are still going to have to get into the wilderness.

This area of southeastern Utah is seemingly all national park and monuments, one after the other, each unique unto itself. This is ancient land revealed, with dinosaur bones, shark's teeth, and fish fossils displaying its inland sea past. The winding rocks and canyons are the product of 300 million years of erosion ranging in formation from the beautiful to the bizarre. There are natural sandstone bridges arching across massive spaces to fields filled with grotesque rocky stumps so lifelike they need only the full moon to start dancing.

From Bryce Canyon's lavender and coral ridges to Zion's

Dick Arentz, Courtesy of Etherton Gallery, Tucson, Arizona

Utah Canyonlands—Bryce Canyon

sheer cliffs, from Arches to the Valley of the Gods to the Valley of the Goblins, round the LaSal Mountain Loop to Dead Horse Point, Utah's Canyonlands are an unforgettable 30,000-square-mile rock fantasy. And you don't have to be a geologist to love it, lithic mania goes with the territory. For more information, write to or call Utah's Canyonlands Region, PO Box 550-C87, Moab, UT 84532; (801) 259-8825.

The following three sites are part of the Utah Canyonlands.

Rainbow Bridge National Monument

Rainbow Bridge is known to many of us as one of the seven natural wonders of the world. It is the Earth's largest natural bridge. Rising out of Lake Powell 290 feet high and 270 feet across, gracefully stretching from one canyon side to the next, it sends the sternest heart fluttering, even if only for a second. It is an inescapable natural response, a reflex.

Rainbow Bridge is a sacred site on many levels. The very shape of it begs a bridge to the supernatural world, as though going through it, physically or astrally, would bring the seeker to another side. Rainbow Bridge, without doubt, is a doorway.

It is a site of particular sacred bearing to the Navajo. These remote canyons were good to those who fled here to escape the flames of Kit Carson's cavalry. Here the survivors joined their brothers near one of their holiest shrines. Oddly enough, Rainbow Bridge was not renamed by the white man, but simply translated from the Navajo.

Rainbow Bridge is the sacred home of the Rainbow God and Spirits, also referred to as Rainbow People. In their religion, it is the Rainbow People who bring forth the rain that cools and nurtures the dry land, grows the crops, and hence feeds the people and animals. Rain and its importance to the people of the desert plateau cannot be overstated. It is the life blood of the land. In this respect, Rainbow Bridge also represents a Guardian of the Universe.

Rain, however, does not go anywhere without clouds. Should you visit Rainbow Bridge, look to the left to see a wide, low-crested mountain in the near distance. It is Navajo Mountain, sacred to them as protector and bringer of clouds. They call it Naatsis'aan, or Head of Earth. Thus, Rainbow Bridge and Head of Earth, in response to prayers and offerings, work together to see that the people are fed.

Many Native American tribes believe that in very ancient times humans lived together with their gods. People, like the gods themselves, were able to change their physical shape and become various animal people or spirits, then change back. When the gods chose to live in a different plane from humans, the latter lost their ability to metamorphose and became locked in their respective animal or human shapes. Today, the great shamans are still able to do the shape-changing magic and once again become animal people.

The notion wherein physical shape is malleable and not of concrete importance for spiritual beings is uncannily similar to esoteric doctrine about the people of the ancient lost civilization of Lemuria. They were not confined to physical shape either, but transformed or resurrected their bodily matter into animal, plant, and spirit and back again as desired.

So whether lost Lemurian or Native American spirit, if you run into a Rainbow Person, do not be surprised and do show some reverence. Surely stranger things have happened at Rainbow Bridge.

Rainbow Bridge can be reached in two ways: by boat from Wahweap or Bullfrog marinas on Lake Powell or by trail. Unless you have your own boat and can wend your way through the 96 canyons of Lake Powell, you can take one of the half- or full-day boat tours. The tours include a stop at Rainbow Bridge and sometimes pass close to Navajo Mountain, which borders the lake. The boat tour is beautiful, but you are then confined to the tour's time schedule (about one hour at Rainbow Bridge) and the group's wiles. The other way in is by trail, which you can do on foot or horseback. There are a number of trails in the Glen Canyon National Recreation Area, but the most popular two are the 14-mile trail from the Navajo Mountain Trading Post and the 13-mile trail from the abandoned Rainbow Lodge. If you're a veteran hiker who prefers more isolation, ask a ranger about other trails. The good part about hiking in is being able to slow down and spend a little time communing with Rainbow Bridge, Navajo Mountain, and the canyons. Every step, bend, and curve offers something new. Late spring and early fall are the prime months for exploring this region. Hiking and horseback permits are required from the Navajo Tribe; write to or call the Navajo Parks and Recreation Department, Window Rock, AZ 86515; (602) 871-6636. For more infomation, contact Glen Canyon National Recreation Area, Box 1507, Page, 86040; (602) 645-2511.

Hovenweep National Monument

A few hours' drive from Rainbow Bridge is Hovenweep, an inspired Anasazi village unique among all the others. Resting half in Utah and half in Colorado, Hovenweep is a group of six Anasazi settlements built high on the canyon tops. Unlike cliff dwellings or many of the larger pueblos, Hovenweep's freestanding architecture features many castlelike towers. These towers are multishaped, built in circles, squares, ovals, and D shapes.

The Hovenweep Anasazi originally lived in open valleys, beginning about A.D. 800, but moved to the cliff-top setting to be closer to their precious source of water, the canyon's springs. Time has ravaged Hovenweep, yet the masonry is so durable that many of the walls still stand, even though some of the mortar has disappeared.

It has long been believed that the towers were used primarily as fortresses, to guard the land and villages, the same as European castles. However, this is questionable; even though the Anasazi seemed to treasure remote locations, there's little or no evidence of battles or weaponry. However, another function has come to light through the work of archaeoastronomers. It appears so far that several buildings at Hovenweep were first rate astronomical stations used at minimum to set up solar calendars. Doing careful and painstaking work at Hovenweep, archaeoastronomer Ray Williamson and his team discovered four buildings there that were used for sky-watching.

At Hovenweep Castle, they discovered at ground level, behind the D-shaped tower, a rubble-filled room that had portholes built into the walls. It is through these ports that the sun triggers some remarkable shadow plays on the walls and doorways of the room during the summer and winter solstices and fall and spring equinoxes. The room may have been designed solely for these purposes.

Thirty-five miles away in Hovenweep, another settlement proved to have an even more complicated system. Here at Cajon, they discovered that the sun's interaction with two separate buildings together revealed the calendar. The shadow dance between the two buildings caused by the movements of the sun projected a giant sundial. Figuring this out required quite a mental leap as nothing like this has been discovered elsewhere in the Southwest. There is, however, a similar interplay between buildings in the ancient Mayan city of Chichén Itzá that Williamson recognized.

Unit-type House, not far from Hovenweep Castle, was also discovered to be designed to pick up solar alignments.

Hovenweep lies in ruin and rubble. Yet the Anasazi's architecture of the sun and these calendrical discoveries are only the beginning, a bare tip of the iceberg that will hopefully someday reveal their world and their vast knowledge, scientifically and spiritually.

Hovenweep National Monument shared by Utah and Colorado; is 17 miles north of Aneth, Utah, on Route 262 at the southeastern corner of Utah and the southwestern corner of Colorado. The roads leading in and around Hovenweep are mostly dirt. It is open year-round and there is a campground at the site. For more information, write to or call Mesa Verde National Park, McElmo Rt., Cortez, CO 81321; (303) 529-4465.

Newspaper Rock State Park Monument, Utah

After you've taken a spin around the twenty-mile Blue Mountain loop in the Manti-LaSal National Forest and are heading toward Canyonlands, take a detour to Indian Creek (a creek, not a town) to see one of the most outrageous collections of ancient pictographs in North America. Newspaper Rock displays several hundred rock art figures, ranging from the sublime to the ridiculous. It is also the product of successive time periods. Some of the carvings date back fifteen centuries, others just a couple of hundred years.

The Newspaper Rock carvings are wholly mysterious. They could be anything from the most profound information on survival in the area to mindless doodling, from spiritual and extraterrestrial visitations to a clan signature, an ancient "Kilroy was here." Hands as they appear in Anasazi petroglyphs are believed to connote prayer or to mark the artwork as sacred. On Newspaper Rock, the recurring theme is feet, with a few of them having six toes. Judaculla Rock in North Carolina (see chapter 5) also features six- and seven-digit hands and feet. We can only speculate as to whom or what these six-toed feet belonged to. Certainly, Newspaper Rock raises a lot more questions than answers, and no one has succeeded in breaking the code. It says something for sure, and some of it could be very enlightening. But for now it stays beyond our grasp.

To reach **Newspaper Rock State Historical Monument**
take U.S. 191 out of Moab, Utah, traveling 40 miles south,
and take a right (or go west) on Route 211. Drive 36 miles
into the park. There is a campground on a first come, first
served, basis. For more information, write to or call the Utah
State Park Southeast Region Office, 125 West, 200 South
Moab, UT 84532; (801) 259-8151.

The Hopi Indian Reservation, Arizona

Somewhere near the spot where the Little Colorado River
empties into the Colorado in the Grand Canyon, the mysterious Hopi Indians emerged into this, the Fourth World,
from the Third. So goes the legend. Wherever they originated, the Hopi people also brought into our world a strik-
ing and powerful spirituality marked by an uncanny pro-
phetic ability. Their shamans seem to be gifted with second
sight.

Their prophecies, recorded on stone tablets, were and are
detailed accounts of the future. They include the "horseless
chariots" that would roll on "black snakes" across the land,
along with the landing of man on the moon. They correctly
predicted numerous aspects of World War II, including the
rising sun of Japan and the use of the reverse swastika by
the Nazis, as well as some grim predictions for humanity
and the Earth in times to come.

It is believed that the Hopi along with the Zuni, Acoma,
and other tribes of the Pueblo tradition are direct descendants of the Anasazi. They give us a glimpse into the world
of their forebears, a world as powerfully complex in some
ways as it was pure and simple in others. For the Anasazi as
it is today for the Hopi, the spiritual side of existence is
woven inextricably into daily life. During times of prosperity,
the Anasazi put even more effort into building great kivas
and amphitheaters for ceremonial worship. Today the Hopi
also put much of their income and creativity into their
religious practices, often called *dances*.

Seeing Hopiland, the visitor might be struck by the lack

of technology and modernization in the villages. Furthermore, the Hopi don't bother with bright-colored clothing or elaborate jewelry like many other southwesterners, native and otherwise. Yet to hear the penetrating sounds of their chants and see the Hopi perform their chilling Snake Dance or any other of their ceremonies is to experience something so visually dazzling and riveting it challenges the most colorful folk spectacles of the world. At minimum it is the greatest of theater, but it is also far more because it is an expression of the power of spirit. This metamorphosis, from the mundane to the mystical, which is the hallmark of true shamanism, is completely misunderstood by our society, which so often judges the unknown solely and soullessly by what it looks like. Native American spirituality is more than misunderstood. It is so completely mysterious we pretend it doesn't exist.

The Hopi settled in the high desert mesas of northern Arizona. Though bands of them moved around and lived elsewhere in the Southwest, they ultimately returned, pure in blood, to the land of their mothers and fathers. Since the tenth century, probably longer, the Hopi have lived on the same land.

Today the Hopi Indian Reservation is a tract of approximately 632,000 acres included within Navajoland. On soil the Anglos have deemed forbidding and impossible, the Hopis have eked out their existence and have even thrived on the gifts given to them by this dry earth. It is because the land appears as it does to outsiders that the Hopi have managed to keep it all. Were their mesas to turn into green fields tomorrow, they might lose them or themselves. Similar to the Anasazi, the Hopis still live in close contact with each other in multidwelling communities, with the exception of a few of their ranchers.

The isolation of Hopiland and the people's connection to it has also protected them. The Spanish soldiers and Franciscan missionaries were pushed out during the 1680 Pueblo Revolt against the invaders. When the invaders returned, they did not reenter. Nevertheless, war, conflict,

Hopi Bean Dance Mask

and attempts to reconquer the Hopi caused political hawk-vs.-dove divisions among the Hopi themselves, resulting in battles and death in the early seventeenth century. There was more trouble from outsiders as well, including Navajo and Apache raids, though nothing matched the death toll brought about by the Anglos' ultimate weapon, smallpox. In the last few centuries, the Hopi have dwindled in number to near extinction several times but have always recovered. Today, they number about ten thousand people or, as they would say, ten thousand souls.

The U.S. created the Hopi Indian Reservation in 1882. Because the Hopi have never been at war with the United States, there have never been any treaties. Like many of the southwestern tribes, with the exception of the Apache, they were spared deportation to the Oklahoma area, if not much else.

The Hopi have to be admired for retaining their priorities and integrity through so much strife. They've had their religion for a thousand years, even longer counting the culture of the Anasazi. It is little wonder that they, like many other Indian peoples, have turned their backs on conversion, even at the price of the missionary's whip. Though many Native Americans now attend Christian churches or their own Native American church, they often combine their new religion with the old ways that are so much a part of their lives.

The Hopi recognize and cherish that they have maintained their cultural identity through the last several centuries of struggle while other native cultures were irreconcilably diluted. It is why to this day they are very careful about visitors, putting much consideration into the value of tourist dollars should they come at the cost of their integrity and lifestyle. And it is why this decades-old sign appears on the road to Old Oraibi: "WARNING: No outside white visitors allowed because of your failure to obey the laws of our tribe as well as your own. This village is hereby closed."

The Hopi command respect on the part of visitors. Every square inch of their land is considered sacred, and they ask for the same respect from anyone who steps on it. The land comprises the Sacred Circle of the Hopi World, where they shall live until their entry into the next universe. The land may appear dry and desolate, but this is an illusion and may even be a bit of a trick for those who live only on the material plane. The truth is that the whole place is spiritually rich and loaded and affects even the most unassuming visitor. The Hopi are a people not to be underestimated. Their religious and cultural ways include experiences that outsiders can only hope to read about or see as tourists, much less aspire to.

The Hopi live on three high mesas, all jutting southward from a great ridge of land called the Black Mesa, which is over six-thousand feet high.

First Mesa. This mesa features Walpi, a village the Hopi have occupied since it was built in 1680 after the Pueblo Revolt. Perched on the tip of the mesa, Walpi towers sixty stories over the surrounding land. The Hopi ask that no photographs be taken or drawings made of Walpi without permission. Other villages on the First Mesa include Tewa (also called Hano) and Sitchomovi. There are two trading posts at the foot of the mesa in Polacca.

Second Mesa. This mesa features the new Hopi Cultural Center. There are also a number of gift and craft shops that sell beautiful Hopi silvercraft, jewelry, woven goods, and the famed kachina dolls. The village of Mishongnovi, founded in the twelfth century, is where the Snake Dance takes place in odd-numbered years. Also in Mishongnovi is the Corn Rock, a sacred shrine for the Hopi where you will see many offerings placed by them. Two other villages, Shipaulovi and Shungopovi, are also on the Second Mesa. Each one has its own rich history. The Snake Dance is held at Shungopavi in the Second Mesa during even-numbered years. Of all the Hopi ceremonies, the Snake Dance is one of the most sacred. The Snake Dance is for rain and the prosperity it brings. In 1923, government agents went on a campaign to ban the Snake Dance, pointing out that the Hopi shouldn't take what they saw as a week's vacation in summer, when they should be working the fields. It didn't seem to occur to them that they were talking about a religious celebration. They tried to push the Hopi into moving the Snake Dance to winter, when there were no crops to tend. This was either a very sly or very dumb move, being that snakes hibernate. Either way, their efforts failed, and the Snake Dance, today as always, takes place sometime in August.

Old Oraibi. This astounding and ancient village, which has been inhabited since A.D. 1100, is on the Third Mesa. It is considered to be the longest-inhabited town in North America. As with Walpi, no photography or drawing is allowed out of respect for the residents. Special permission can be obtained from the village's leader. However, the village is not always closed to visitors. Check ahead. Near to Old Oraibi are Kyakotsmovi, where tribal headquarters are, and the villages of Hotevilla, Bacabi, and Moencopi.

There are two camping areas on the Hopi Indian Reservation and one new motel on the Second Mesa. Should you stay overnight, take some time to do some sky-watching.

The sky in this high desert area is brilliantly clear. The stars and planets are luminous and multicolored, almost touchable, and satellites can be seen spinning overhead. It is easy for a soul to fly here.

The Hopi hold numerous ceremonies and sacred rituals throughout the year. During the summer months ceremonies are held about once a week. Not all of them are serious. Many Native American sacred dances include levity, clowns, and laughter; in a word, they are joyous. The Snake Dance is a mesmerizing ceremony done with live rattlers, racers, and bull snakes, and the Hopi graciously assure that no visitor has ever been bitten during a Snake Dance. Portions of some of these ceremonies are open to the public. Naturally, there are some rituals so exclusive that only the initiated among the tribe are allowed to be present.

Tawa, the Hopi Sun Kachina representing life, illumination, and happiness.

A famed feature of southwestern art and Indian religion is Hopi (and Zuni) in origin, the kachinas. The kachinas are deities or spirits in the Hopi religion. There are several hundred different kachinas, ranging from clowns and benevolent angels to evil spirits that wreak havoc. There are two manifestations of the kachinas in our physical world. First, they are often personified by dancers in full costume in ceremony. The second manifestation of the kachinas is in the form of beautiful dolls, which are used as educational tools to teach children the different spirits and their religious meaning. Kachinas are made by both the Hopi and Zuni Indians and are sold commercially. Because they are so beautiful, there are numerous cheap copies, so check around for authenticity. At present the Hopi are obtaining their own trademark to protect buyers and sellers of kachina dolls.

The **Hopi Reservation** is in the northeastern part of Arizona within Navajoland, south of the Navajo National Monument area. Route 264 traverses the three mesas east to west. Route 87 leads to the Second Mesa from Winslow, Arizona, which is 65 miles south. Guided tours can be arranged through the Hopi Public Relations Office. For more information, write to or call the Hopi Tribal Council, Public Relations, PO Box 123, Kyakotsmovi, AZ 86039; (602) 734-2441.

Montezuma's Castle, Arizona

Seeing some of the cliff dwellings of the ancient Southwest can produce a very out-of-balance feeling after a while. You are either looking up at them as they loom high over your head or leaning over cliffsides to get a closer view of them far below. Either way, there's a tremendous feeling of distance between their world and ours. The same urge that you feel to jump into the world of a painting or storybook is at play here. It is the urge to leap above or over the crags and cliffs into their world through time and space. As it is, the ruins seem to beckon from afar. Unfortunately but understandably, visitors are not allowed inside many of the ruins, in order to preserve them.

The true inaccessibility of these cliffside castles boggles the mind. It would seem that the residents were trying to protect themselves from something, maybe marauding bandits or simply the sun and wind. Nevertheless, archaeology indicates that these were peaceful agricultural societies that flourished for several centuries. All the same, for them to leave their homes and get back again seems a death-defying feat, ladders or not.

Montezuma's Castle is one of the prettiest and well-preserved cliff dwellings located in a spiritually rich area of central Arizona called the Verde Valley. Footpaths lead to the cliff dwelling area from where you can stare up at this tucked-away five-story structure containing twenty rooms. It is gracefully built, following the curve of the hillside. That it has survived with minimal repairs for about seven hundred years despite the elements and reckless looting of artifact hunters, is a tribute to the castle's remarkable builders.

One of the first things to know about Montezuma's Castle is that it has nothing to do with Montezuma, the great Aztec sovereign. It's a complete misnomer. The first white settlers in the area were so impressed by it that they decided it must have been an outpost for the Mexican king and named it accordingly. An exciting idea, but hardly the case.

In 1065, a volcano in northern Arizona, now called Sunset Crater, erupted and covered the land with an ash layer. Rather than ruining the soil, the ash layer protected it from the sun so it retained moisture and became rich for farming. What followed was an eleventh-century land rush to the area, and many of the Hohokam people in the central Verde Valley moved north.

In the meantime, a group of Sinagua from the north, who were probably sick of the crowds, moved south into the valley left behind. The Sinagua stayed there through several hundred years, building Montezuma's Castle during this time. They irrigated the land and grew several different crops, along with cotton that they wove into beautiful cloth-

Scott Peterson

Montezuma's Castle

ing and other goods they traded. They also mined and traded salt. They didn't excel in pottery but in weaving and crafts. It is still possible to see their irrigation canals. The lime in the water eventually hardened, lining the canals with a cementlike substance that survives today. Some of these canals have been reconstructed and are still used.

About eight miles from the castle is Montezuma's Well, a lush oasis in this dry area. It is a 400-foot-wide limestone sink fed by an underground spring. The water flows constantly, over a million gallons a day. Nearby are more Sinaguan and some Hohokam ruins that housed several hundred people.

The Sinagua abandoned the valley in the early fifteenth

century. Another group, the contemporary Yavapai Indians, were living there when the Spanish arrived almost two hundred years later.

The Verde Valley and nearby Sedona red rock area are very sacred to the Yavapai. They believe Montezuma's Well was the gate through which they entered this world. Later, when it filled with water, the water was considered holy.

Montezuma's Castle and **Montezuma's Well** are off Interstate 17, which runs north-south through the center of the state. It is near Camp Verde, about 90 miles north of Phoenix. For more information write or call to, Superintendent, Montezuma's Castle National Monument, PO Box 219, Camp Verde, AZ 86322; (602) 567-3322.

Tuzigoot National Monument, Arizona

Across the Verde Valley area, twenty-five miles from the Montezuma's Castle area, is an imposing stone and mud building atop a long ridge. Originally two or three stories high in places, this mansion village had seventy-seven rooms on the ground floor alone. In its heyday, Tuzigoot supported several hundred people. It is built on top of a long ridge that is 120 feet higher than the surrounding land. Here the residents could see for miles around them and be protected from occasional floods on the northern side of the valley. Tuzigoot, like all names for ancient Americans, is a modern word. It is Apache for "crooked water," referring to the nearby Verde River, which snakes through the region.

Like Montezuma's Castle, Tuzigoot was originally Hohokam and later was taken over by Sinaguan farmers. Its height and later abandonment also occurred during the same times as at Montezuma's Castle. Centuries later, in the 1930s, the clearing and preservation of both sites were done by the same University of Arizona archaeological group. Much of it was salvage excavation and repairs.

What separates the two sites are their architecture and structural materials. Tuzigoot does not have the same enduring qualities as Montezuma's Castle. Keeping it from crumbling under the elements is a constant task for its caretakers.

As you walk around or meditate at either Montezuma's Castle or Tuzigoot, attune not only to the ruins, but to the land itself. Equidistant from both sites, about 20 miles north, is reputedly one of the most intense power spots on the planet, Sedona (see the following site).

Tuzigoot National Monument is open weekdays all year long, 8 A.M. to 7 P.M. Memorial Day through Labor Day and 8 A.M. to 5 P.M. the rest of the year. Take Route 279 off Interstate 17 or Alternate Route 89 into Clarkdale. The site is 2 miles east. For more information, write Tuzigoot, P.O. Box 68, Clarkdale, AZ 86324, or call the visitor center/ museum at (602) 634-5564.

Sedona and Oak Creek Canyon, Arizona

If you have been working with crystals in private, or feeling a little lonely about that telepathic dream you had that you judiciously didn't tell anyone about, or found yourself in the astral plane during your last meditation, go to Sedona and you won't be lonely any longer. You'll meet other people who are just as involved with psychic ability and spiritual development. For good reasons, Sedona is becoming a focal point, a New Age Mecca so to speak, for metaphysical ideas and exploration. Sedona is known to be a point of particularly strong vibration on the Earth's energy matrix. For those psychically attuned, a trip to Sedona could mean a paranormal field day. If you're not oriented toward this sort of work, the energy boost inherent in Sedona can and often does promote a terrific feeling. It's true even for people who are completely unaware of Sedona in this way. All they know is that they are powerfully attracted to this gorgeous place and hope to return again.

Occasionally, on the other hand, it can be too much. This brings up a salient point. Most sacred sites have something for everyone, but not always. If nothing else, their quiet beauty touches a chord in nearly all humans that rarely misses. But sometimes, they can stir up different feelings and sensations in people, from the most sublime peacefulness to downright agitation. Blending and matching your own energy with the site is important. It's another reason why we often develop personal relationships with different sites.

A friend of mine who spent a lot of time in the Northwest said he really didn't like Sedona very much. It made him uncomfortable. I was very surprised; it was the first time I had ever heard that somebody disliked Sedona. I asked him about it. He stated simply, "Too much red." "Too much red?" Further prodding brought out the full explanation.

It was late autumn, and the dry wind gave the shrubbery and trees that dotted the landscape a parched yellowish cast. He had arduously hiked up one of the buttes where he could rest and mindlessly take in the spectacular view and oncoming sunset. But instead of peacefully drifting, he found himself instead in a highly irritated state. He began observing his surroundings with a searing clarity. The vegetation was dry and made crackling sounds in the wind; the ground itself was a glowing brick-red color. Before him in the distance were 180 degrees of vibrant red rocks and buttes. As the sun set, the sky quickly deepened into a fiery array of hot orange, yellow, and purple. Even if he closed his eyes, the reds seemed to penetrate right into him as if there were no escape. Despite the drop in temperature, he felt hotter, flushed. He drank the rest of the water in his canteen and moved into the nearest patch of shade. He waited until the sky turned a velvety dark blue to descend.

A few days later he was back in Oregon, where, surrounded by dark green timberland and a misty sky, he breathed a cool sigh of relief. He laughed, thinking about how depressed a red rock person would get under the same pearl-gray skies he loved.

Too much red. It overstimulated him. Sedona is a ruby of the Earth, and like rubies, it connects to the heart center and works on the emotions.

The point is, if you are very sensitive to lively energy, at minimum bring a good pair of shades. Sedona is unsubtle. Red, blue, green, yellow—all the colors of the spectrum take on a dramatic glow in her aura. It is little wonder Hollywood gravitated to Sedona.

Seeing Sedona in person for the first time brings an inevitable smile of recognition. We've seen it at least a dozen times, if not on the silver screen, then for sure on our television sets. So many western movies were shot there that for decades the second profession to ranching for locals was appearing as cowboys in the movies.

Sedona's creative allure has also tantalized many of the West's most talented sculptors and painters for decades. It was and still is famous as an artists' colony. Among those who made Sedona their home was the great surrealist Max Ernst. As a growing art center, her numerous galleries feature both traditional and modern artworks, with an emphasis on the spirit of the West.

Sedona is neither an Indian nor a Spanish name. It belonged to a very pretty dark-eyed woman from Missouri, who was named by her Pennsylvanian Dutch mother. Sedona Schnebly moved to the area with her husband in 1901. When they applied to the government for a post office, the name Schnebly Station was ruled out. It was named after Sedona instead. Sedona is also an anagram for the word *anodes*, or positive electrodes. The original Greek meaning is even more enticing. It means "a way up" and there are numerous ways "up" in Sedona. The following four spots are renowned psychic vortexes brought to contemporary consciousness primarily through the work of psychic Dick Sutphen. Whatever their charged history, they are being reempowered in the present by today's ardent seekers.

Cathedral Rock. Cathedral Rock is one of the most photographed western spots ever. It rises a thousand feet above the surrounding terrain. Light does funny things to Cathedral Rock. During sunset, it often appears to be glowing from within, and it probably is.

Bell Rock. Truly beautiful as it looks down upon the village of Oak Creek, Bell Rock appears to be glowing and singularly removed from the surrounding buttes. It is purportedly the site of much UFO activity over the years and has a beacon quality that, like a psychic telephone, facilitates communication with higher beings.

Airport Mesa. Airport Mesa is highly charged with electrical currents. It's a good place to feel your hair stand on end.

Boynton Canyon. Serene and powerful, Boynton Canyon will at minimum fulfill its promise as one of the best walks you'll ever know. More than that, however, is the canyon's balanced energy, which enhances creativity and psychic endeavors. Boynton Canyon is a very sacred place to the Yavapai Indians. According to their lore, after the land was last destroyed by flood, one woman survived the disaster. She was First Woman and lived in a cave in Boynton Canyon. There First Woman became pregnant by Sun and Cloud and gave birth to a great leader of the Yavapai.

These four places have a reputation for being psychic vortexes. However, should you find your feet or intuition leading you elsewhere, follow the call. There are many rocks, ridges, and buttes in Sedona and adjacent Oak Creek Canyon that beg for exploration and experimentation. Don't confine yourself to one vortex if an inner pull leads you elsewhere.

To reach **Sedona**, take the marked exit off Interstate 17, which runs north-south through central Arizona. Sedona is approximately a two-hour drive north of Phoenix. Sedona and Oak Creek are combinations of towns, parks, and private land. Become aware of which is which. The best way is via the area's visitor center, called Visitor's Guide. There are also Jeep tours that will guide and take you around. This is a region of desert animals, including cougars and coyotes, rattlers, and even tarantulas. Keep in mind that the old maxim generally holds true: they are more afraid of you than you are of them. For more information, write to or call Visitor's Guide, 431 Route 179, Sedona, AZ 86336, (602) 282-9022; or the Chamber of Commerce, Forest Rd. and Route 89A, Sedona, AZ 86336; (602) 282-7722.

"Show Me the Magic"

Chuck is a soundtrack composer and video artist who often visits wilderness areas. His first trip to Sedona held a few surprises for him.

"I went to Arizona on a camping trip because I was depressed. I had broken up with my girlfriend and really missed her. I couldn't get over it, and nothing helped. I needed to get outdoors and just camp, figuring it might help me get out of the rut I was in. I had heard Sedona was pretty country and read about some UFO stuff, but that was about it. So I packed up my motorcycle and left L.A.

"For four days I camped here and there but couldn't shake the depression and started thinking I should go home. I got to Sedona on the full moon and went in on a side road. That night I camped near a place called Loy Butte, and even though it rained awhile that night, I suddenly realized that I felt a little lighter, like the clouds over me had lifted a little. I walked up to a nearby Indian ruin, and the moonlight was very bright. The coyotes were singing everywhere. I sat near the ruin, and in a joking, sarcastic way I said, 'Okay, show me the magic.' Immediately, instantly from the distance a loud, sharp buzzing noise came right at me and flew past me. I broke out in goose bumps. I'd never felt or heard anything like it. I looked up and saw this image, I guess you could say ghost, but it was different. I saw this four-foot-tall medicine man doing this fast, outrageous dance. I picked up feelings immediately that he was frightened, but also angry at me. I felt that I was invading his world. I looked away and back, and he was still there. I closed my eyes, and when I opened them he was gone. I figured my imagination was in top form and returned to my tent.

"The next day I went into town and bought a book on Sedona's hiking trails. In one of the bookstores I saw a book on the psychic vortexes, Dick Sutphen Presents

Sedona: Psychic Energy Vortexes, *and looked at it. That's when I realized that a lot of people see Indian spirits there, and I felt vindicated about what I had seen. The rest of my stay was more emotional than anything else. In Boynton Canyon I received the emotional release I had needed, and my depression simply washed away. For the first time in months I felt joy again. Everything was lifted off me, and for the next five days time merged together into one moment. I forgot about everything I was worried about. It was so good to feel good again, even though I hated to leave.*

"When I got home, I took off my dirty hiking boots and didn't put them on again for several days. When I did, all the Sedona dust was still on them. All of a sudden, it felt like my boots were alive, as though bolts of energy were shooting off them. It was great. It was a reminder that what I had gotten in Sedona was still with me."

Navajoland, Arizona

Unlike the tribes of the Pueblo tradition, who are direct descendants of the Anasazi, the forebears of both the Navajo and the Apache migrated into the area from Canada somewhere around the thirteenth century. There must have been some interplay between the two peoples, but not enough for the Navajo to lose their own identity. They remained primarily nomadic clans, not easily given to settling down and farming.

Quick and enterprising, the Navajo, who call themselves the Dineh, or the People, soon picked up sheepherding and weaving from the Pueblos, along with other religious and tribal practices. Their relationship with neighboring tribes was alternately marked by raids and peaceful trading. From the Spanish, they learned horsemanship. For 265 years beginning with Spanish and subsequent U.S. rule over the Southwest, the Navajo were never subdued. They were great warriors. The frightened and frustrated white settlers in the Southwest called them the "Lords of the Earth."

In 1863, Colonel Kit Carson was dispatched to break them. Foreshadowing Sherman's Run through the South a few years later during the Civil War, Kit Carson set upon Navajo territory and burned everything: fields, sheep, livestock, and houses. Some escaped into the high country, but most of them were starved into submission. Those who surrendered took "The Long Walk," which still figures so prominently in Navajo consciousness. Eight thousand Navajo men, women, and children walked to the Ft. Sumner prisoner-of-war camp three hundred miles away in eastern New Mexico. Many perished en route or in the camp. The experiment to "convert and reeducate" the Navajo proceeded. Four years later it was declared a failure, and an 1868 treaty returned part of their homelands to them as a reservation. In 1923, they formed their own tribal council and since that time have managed to expand their reservation lands three times. Today there are eighty-eight elected delegates to the council as well as the chairman and vice-chariman. The center for the council is in Window Rock, Arizona.

Navajoland is filled with sacred sites and power spots. It is noteworthy that although they lived in and among ancient places for hundreds of years, they did nothing to alter or harm them out of respect for "the Ancient Ones" and their spirits. It took but a few decades of white vandals, swarming over these sacred sites like so many locusts, to eat away their secrets forever.

Navajoland (which also geographically includes the Hopi Reservation) has much to offer. For more information about tribal celebrations, trading posts, and camping, write to or call the Navajoland Tourism Office, Navajo Nation, PO Box 308, Window Rock, AZ 86515; (602) 871-4941.

The following five sites are all part of Navajoland, maintained in conjunction with state and national park services.

Lawrence McFarland, Courtesy of Etherton Gallery, Tucson, Arizona

Navajo Reservation—The End of the Road

Canyon de Chelly, Arizona

Canyon de Chelly (pronounced "de shay") is a sacred site doubly empowered by a magical natural setting and several hundred Anasazi ruins. Unlike other sites that were occupied and then abandoned, Canyon de Chelly has been attracting people to its secluded red sandstone walls since A.D. 300 or longer. It has been the setting for five different eras of southwestern history. No visitor leaves silent, beautiful, and secluded de Chelly feeling the same way she or he arrived. It is a place that practically guarantees the surrender of tension and inner renewal. Canyon de Chelly bears the reputation of being a power source. If so, much of this power includes clearing and healing.

Like Sedona and Oak Creek, Canyon de Chelly is one of several red rock canyons in Arizona, along with the adjacent Monument Canyon and Canyon del Muerto. De Chelly is twenty-six miles long and attaches to Canyon del Muerto, which is thirty-five miles long. The canyon walls rise up to a thousand feet above the canyon floor. The walls of the canyon are so steep and smooth they look as if they were cut and shaped by a potter's knife.

The Anasazi lived in Canyon de Chelly for a thousand years, growing corn, beans, and squash at the bottom of the canyon and hunting in the pine forest above. This is when most of the ruins that line the canyon were built. Their descendants intermittently drifted in and out of the canyon. There is some evidence that the Hopi lived there for a while, with major occupation occurring again when the Navajo moved during the early 1700s. Beautiful Navajo pictographs can still be seen on canyon walls. In the canyon the Navajo felt safe from encroachment and friction with the Spanish military and missionaries. But not for long. In 1805, a day-long battle with the Spanish claimed 130 Navajo lives in the canyon that gave Massacre Cave in Canyon del Muerto its name. Canyon de Chelly would never be safe again. In 1863 Canyon de Chelly fell to Kit Carson, marking the turning point in Navajo resistance.

Canyon de Chelly was returned to the Navajo in the 1868 treaty, which defined reservation lands. For reasons of protection against desecration, the National Park Service took over in the 1920s. At that time, a tough archaeologist named Earl Morris, along with several work teams, took on the task of salvage excavation and careful, sensitive reconstruction of many of de Chelly's ruins. Today Canyon de Chelly is once again under the aegis of the Navajo Nation in conjunction with the park service. Navajo farmers and ranchers have made it their home again.

Besides the entire place, there are five spots of note:

The White House Ruins. This is a beautiful Anasazi cliff dwelling built under a huge, sheer cliff that hangs ominously over it.

Antelope House. Antelope House is an Anasazi house named for the colorful wall paintings done there by a Navajo artist 150 years ago.

The Mummy Cave. One of the oldest and finest extant Anasazi ruins, it dates back to A.D. 300. It was named for the naturally desiccated bodies that archaeologists found in the cave.

Spider Rock. Another of those outrageous geological wonders so typical to this land, this site is an 800-foot-high narrow rock tower rising from the canyon floor.

Standing Cow Ruin. There are many prehistoric and Navajo pictographs throughout the canyon, but Standing Cow is wonderful, painted in blue and white. There is also a painting of the Spanish cavalry accompanied by a priest.

Canyon de Chelly and **Canyon del Muerto** are part of Navajo country. Canyon de Chelly is restricted Navajo land. This protects the canyon from being overrun and helps to maintain its pristine atmosphere. It also makes visiting a bit complicated. The park is open from April through October. There is one self-guided 2½-mile trail that leads to an overlook view of the White House Ruins. There are also two drives around the canyon's rim: South Rim Drive, which is 36 miles round-trip, and North Rim Drive, which is 34 miles round-trip. There are overlooks along the way from which you'll see many of the canyon's most important features, though at a distance.

To descend into the canyon or do any camping there, you must be accompanied by an authorized Navajo guide or park ranger and have a permit. You also must have four-wheel drive. All this can be arranged in advance. Thunderbird Lodge near the monument's headquarters in Chinle also arranges Jeep trips into the canyon. There is also camping near the monument headquarters. Do not let any of these rules or regulations stymie your plans to visit Canyon de Chelly or other areas in the southwestern high country. Once you are there you'll wonder how you might have ever considered missing it.

Three highways lead to the park: U.S. 191 to the west; Route 64, which borders it to the north; and Route 12 to the east. Monument Headquarters is off U.S. 191. For more information, write to or call the Superintendent, Canyon de Chelly National Monument, Box 588, Chinle, AZ 86503; (602) 674-5436.

Navajo National Monument, Arizona

Navajo National Monument is only one part of Navajo country. Comprising six hundred acres, the monument features two of the largest Anasazi ruins in Arizona, Betatakin and Keet Seel. For aficionados of Anasazi culture, these cliff dwellings are masterpieces made all the more mysterious by their incredible isolation. At an altitude of 7,300 feet, they are as remarkable as the breathtaking land they were built on.

Anasazi culture is divided by three distinct masonry and artistic styles or subcultures: Kayenta, Mesa Verde, and Chaco. All the Arizona cliff dwellings are Kayenta, including Betatakin and Keet Seel. The work of the Kayenta Anasazi tends to be the least elaborate of the three. The people who built and lived in these sites have been connected through their artifacts with the modern Pueblo cultures.

Betatakin. Betatakin (Navajo for "house on the ledge") is the most accessible of the three cliff dwellings in the park (at present one of them is not open to the public). Even at that, getting there takes some work. First there is a guided Jeep ride that will take you to a trail. From there it is a three-mile round-trip walk by guide only. The hike includes a 700-foot descent into the canyon, so climbing back out is the equivalent of walking up a seventy-story building. But the climb back up the canyon isn't nearly as arduous as previously thought. Sometimes people feel like they are floating back up. Obviously the Anasazi were tough and strong. They made the trek up and down the steep canyons perhaps daily. Their water supply and fields were on canyon floors, and hunting expeditions took place above in the deserts and forests.

Descending into a canyon is a special sensation. In this region, the canyons are often cooler and more lush than the dusty country of the high mesas above. A different world unfolds with each step.

Suddenly, beneath a massive cliff overhang appears Betatakin, with 135 rooms built on ledges of varying height. It is so astounding it takes a few seconds to focus, to take it in. Entering the village, one can see the smoky residues of Anasazi cooking fires on the apartment walls. This close, the Anasazi's presence fills the place, and they become very real. What is different about Betatakin is how short its occupancy was. Whereas most of the other Anasazi villages were inhabited for several hundred years, sometimes on and off for a thousand years, Betatakin appears to have housed people for only fifty years, a scant few generations. Surprising when one considers the amount of work required to build it. It was supposedly built over thirty-six years, from A.D. 1250 to 1286, and abandoned about 1300. It is believed the Anasazi abandoned the village when water on the canyon floor ran dry. Yet there must have been other reasons as well. Over the land of the Anasazi, even a couple of hundred miles away, the people were abandoning their villages all about the same time.

Keet Seel. Keet Seel ("broken pottery" in Navajo) takes some work to get to, but in a way that is more involving because it gives a person that much more time to tune into the land and separate from the rest of civilization. It is eight miles from headquarters. You can walk there via an arduous primitive trail or arrange to go by horseback. It can be done in one day, or you can camp overnight in the canyon and return the next day. Guides are required.

Keet Seel was inhabited on and off for 350 years, A.D. 950 to 1300. It lies nestled in an eroded alcove beneath a huge sandstone cliff streaked with red. The ruin appears to have been built by a different group from those who built Betatakin. Though it is Kayenta Anasazi, there are many more kivas for worship, an important thing to the Anasazi, and more architectural variation. Some of the rooms were used as granaries. The peak population of Keet Seel was about 150 people. When the people of Keet Seel left their home, they may have been hoping to return someday. They did something few other Anasazi bothered with: they sealed the doorways behind them.

Due to the sheltering cliffs, Keet Seel and Betatakin are very well preserved. They have a deceivingly new look, betraying the seven hundred years they have been here. It is perhaps what makes the Anasazi people so accessible in Betatakin and Keet Seel. They could have been there in the flesh a few short years ago, not centuries ago. These two ruins bridge the gap.

Inscription House is yet another ruin in the monument. Built in the open like Tuzigoot, it has the same problem of erosion under the elements. Visits into Inscription House are no longer allowed because of this.

An interesting story goes with Inscription House. It is believed that the first whites ever to see Betatakin and Keet Seel were trader John Wetherill and archaeologist Bryan Cummings in 1906. But not so with Inscription House. This pueblo is named after the Spanish explorer who carved his initials and the date 1661 onto one of its walls.

To reach Navajo National Monument, take U.S. 160 50 miles northeast from Tuba City or 20 miles southwest from Kayenta. Route 564 is a 9-mile paved road (many of the roads in the region are dirt) that will take you to the Monument Headquarters. Keet Seel is open in the summer only, from Memorial Day to Labor Day. The Betatakin Overlook is open all year. The nearby campgrounds are open from mid-May to mid-October. Visits to Betatakin can be made only with a park ranger. There are guided tours daily, with never more than 24 people at a time. A visit to Keet Seel requires a permit and is also restricted to 24 people a day. Reservations can be made in advance, and the visitor's center has information about horseback trips. Hours for both sites vary. For more information, write to or call Superintendent, Navajo National Monument, HC 71, Box 3, Tonalea, AZ 86044-9704; (602) 672-2366.

Wupatki National Monument, Arizona

It is appropriate that the Wupatki ruin should have been dug out of a dune of black cinders and rock. The layers of outcropping well represent the many layers of culture and civilization that have trod over Wupatki for a thousand years or more.

So far, Wupatki appears to have been a village consisting of seventy rooms surrounding a great circular ceremonial amphitheater. In 1965 another feature of the village was dug out of fifteen feet of rubble—the ball court. It is only the beginning of Wupatki National Monument's secrets.

Wupatki projects the feeling of being untampered with. Refreshingly, many of the ruins here have yet to be excavated. Spareness in the land on the visual level is one small part of the place. The 35,700-acre park features about 800 ruins and archaeological sites, 127 of them in one square mile alone. Time is condensed here, with centuries of human worship, activity, and survival stacked up in and upon the land before us. Because the ash layer from the eruption of the Sunset Crater volcano made the land fertile for farming, the Wupatki area became heavily populated. Similar to Betatakin, it is believed the Anasazi of this area are direct ancestors of the Hopi people.

After the Anasazi left Wupatki in the early 1300s, the place was inhabited only by transient and quite possibly outlaw groups. There is evidence that the Hopi, Spanish, and other tribes passed through Wupatki, never stopping for long. The first Anglo to mention Wupatki was a Lieutenant Sitgreaves in 1851, who was on an exploring expedition. In the 1930s, an illegal whisky still was being run near the ruin. It was a good thing archaeologists from the Museum of Northern Arizona moved in to start some excavation work. The bootleggers were in the habit of using valuable centuries-old timber from the ruin to fire up the still.

The Wupatki ruin itself (Hopi for "Tall House") impressively contains a hundred rooms. Near the Tall House is an amphitheater for religious ceremonies, the ball court, and "Blow Hole." The Wupatki Blow Hole is a weird opening in one of the underground limestone layers that literally breathes, inhaling and exhaling air that moves through the underground cavities. The breathing is caused by air pressure.

Other important sites at Wupatki include the three-story Wukoki ruin, the Citadel, and Nalakihu. Most of these villages were inhabited for about 150 years, from A.D. 1100 to 1250.

Wupatki National Monument is 35 miles north of Flagstaff, Arizona, on U.S. 89. It is also part of a loop road leading to Sunset Crater. It is open all year during daylight hours. The tours here are self-guided, which makes it easy to be alone for a while in Wupatki. For more information, write to or call Wupatki National Monument, HC 33, Box 44a, Flagstaff, AZ 86001; (602) 527-7040.

Sunset Crater, Arizona

Eighteen miles south of Wupatki is Sunset Crater, the volcano that changed the lives of the surrounding people and land for two centuries. Sunset Crater is an extinct volcano that last erupted in A.D. 1064 to the good of the region. Covering the surrounding dry lands with ash protected it from the harsh sun and gave the ancient southwesterners rich farmlands until a drought once again dried up the land decades later.

Volcanoes are ferocious natural phenomena. As if they were the product of gods who wish to make a powerful statement, volcanoes express nature's rage. Whatever its cool aftermath, a volcano takes on a life of its own, whose unpredictability leaves human hearts uneasy. The ancients made many offerings to Sunset Crater.

Sunset Crater still appears alive, which is how it got its name. Light does funny things to its thousand-foot cone. It appears as though the volcanic cone is in the setting sun, no matter what the hour. It commands the imagination.

The amiable Kana-a kachinas live in Sunset Crater. Hopi legends speak of the many magical and wonderful things they do for people. However, the Wind God, Yaponcha, lives deep below the crater and, through a crack in black lava, blows the white clouds and sands into a fury. It is true that a cold, breathy wind always seems to rise from the bottom of the crater.

Sunset Crater National Monument is off U.S. 89 about 15 miles north of Flagstaff and 18 miles south of Wupatki on Loop Road, which connects the two sites. There are self-guided trails leading to and around the crater. The park has campsites and is open all year except when heavy snows shut it down. The visitor information center is open 8-5 daily; summer hours may be longer. For site hours or other information, write to or call Wupatki-Sunset Crater National Monument, 2717 N. Steves Blvd., Flagstaff, AZ 86001; (602) 527-7042.

Monument Valley Navajo Park, Arizona

No matter how many times you've seen Monument Valley in classic western movies, contemporary videos, commercials, or photographs, being there is an altogether different experience. It is infinitely better. Surrounded by Monument Valley in real time and in real color is jumping right into the storybook land that has inspired so many dreams and visions. One thing is for sure: no human could have designed this place, for this is nature's palette gone wild, creating from dust a panorama that never ceases to dazzle. As long as there are paints and cameras, there will be a picture of Monument Valley nearby. The desire to capture the vision and take it home is irresistible.

To Native Americans, to anyone, Monument Valley is a land of visions, both internal and external. It stimulates creativity and melts away mental barriers. Its isolation in balance with its fanciful beauty is the rush of seeing something for the first time in an unbounded, newly innocent way, like a child's garden of delights. As there are sacred sites that cleanse the heart and comfort the soul, Monument Valley clears the head, zinging out the old, lightening the mind, and rousing the imagination.

The entire Four Corners region is endowed with a reckless rocky beauty made extravagant by simple sunlight. Even at that, Monument Valley is the icing on a cake whose bottom layer is the magnificent Grand Canyon. Prepare to be awestruck, because there is nothing else like it in the world.

As you would watch a cloud-filled sky take on the shape of horses, dragons, and other animals, so it is with Monument Valley. The bizarre rock formations and stone spires take on a life of their own; castles, faces, beasts, and spirits appear in them, ever changing with each new angle and shadow. Swirling storm clouds, snow, or glowing moonlight changes the entire spirit of the place as one visual delight after the next gets heaped on the psyche. It makes sense that many of the individual formations are given names such as the Temple, Emperor on His Throne, Castle Butte, Bear and Rabbit, and Eagle Rock.

Monument Valley is a jewel of the Earth, "the land of room enough and time enough" and a good reflection of the Navajo love of color. The Navajo have lived and pro-

Steven H. Miller

Monument Valley

tected Monument Valley for several hundred years. Even after Canyon de Chelly fell to Kit Carson, the Navajo of Monument Valley were able to save themselves from the Trail of Tears. In 1958, their tribal council wisely set the valley aside as a park to discourage any mining, nuclear testing, or similar activities that were rapidly changing the face and atmosphere of western land. Fortunately, Monument Valley has stayed pristine due to their efforts. Today many Navajo still live in Monument Valley and comprise the park's staff and rangers. They also stick to their traditional lifestyle of living in hogans and sheepherding. When they're not driving their pickups, it's not unusual to see a Navajo treading the land bareback.

They were not, however, the first residents. There are dozens of petroglyphs, Anasazi and pre-Anasazi remains in Monument Valley, particularly in an area called Mystery Valley.

It is asked that you respect the residents' privacy and photograph them or their homes only after getting permission and/or setting a fee.

Monument Valley Navajo Park is in the northeastern corner of Navajoland, and is under their jurisdiction. It is 50 miles from Four Corners Monument. Most of the park is in Arizona on U.S. 163, 22 miles north of Kayenta at the Utah border. There is a campground near the park entrance and accommodations in nearby towns. There is a sixteen-mile loop you can drive through Monument Valley. Off the loop at North Window, walk the short trail to several lookout points for more incredible views. If you have four-wheel drive (you can rent one with a guide/driver at several nearby lodges), you will be able to get off the main paved road for a closer and unhampered visit with the people and panorama of the valley. Four-wheel drive is also handy during rainy weather or snows, which sometimes gut the roads. As at many sacred sites, the silence of Monument Valley is starkly noticeable. For city slickers, it can be a revelation. For more information, write to or call Superintendent, Monument Valley Navajo Park, Box 93, Monument Valley, UT 84536; (801) 727-3287.

Shiprock, New Mexico

There are sacred summits all over the world, named as such by their position on the Earth's energy matrix, surely their proximity to the heavens, and their use by shamans to develop their power. Often these mountains are associated with sacred beings or events, similar to Mt. Olympus for the Greeks or Mt. Sinai in the Judeo-Christian religion. Mt. Cuchama, also known as Mt. Tecati, at the southern border of California near Mexicali, was where Aztec priests challenged each other's power in a literal battle of wizards.

Sacred summits represent more to people than the physical challenge of ascending to the top; they represent spiritual ascension.

So it is with Shiprock, known in Navajo as Tse'bit'a'i. It is a Navajo sacred summit that rises 1,700 feet high above the surrounding land. Its peak is 7,178 feet above sea level. The name in Navajo means "Rock with Wings." This great mountain is a volcanic core, created about thirty million years ago, with jagged rock spreading out from the base. The name is well suited. On a hot summer day in late afternoon, a mirage appears that makes the mountain look as though it is indeed flying above the land.

This illusion is what also got the mountain its white man's name, Shiprock. The early settlers thought it looked like a ship at full sail on the waters the mirage created.

The legend of Shiprock is much like the dragonslayer stories of the Celts. To the Navajo, Shiprock is the mountain where the Slayer of Enemy Gods or Monster Slayer outwitted two terrible flying dragons that had been plaguing the people. Monster Slayer used his magic to ride on a whirling wind to a steep ledge on the mountain where the two hideous creatures, male and female, resided. He cautiously watched as the two monsters took off for the night to do their killing. He looked up to find himself confronted by the monsters' two young and learned from them when their mother and father would return. Monster Slayer then prepared his attack with a magic feather given to him by Spider Woman. When the monsters returned, he killed them with two arrows made of lightning. The young also thought they would be killed, but Monster Slayer spared them. He flung the first and then the second into the sky and changed them into an eagle and an owl. He told them that men would now listen to their voices to know their future. With his work done and the people saved, Monster Slayer had one last dilemma—how to get off the mountain. But then Bat Woman appeared and brought him safely to level land.

Other legends say that Shiprock was once a great bird from the north turned into the mountain or that it was once a monster turned by magic into stone.

Shiprock is a sacred place to the Navajo, and although some climbers have attempted to scale it, the Navajo prefer that no one climb it.

Shiprock Peak is 15 miles southwest of the city of Ship-rock, New Mexico, off Route 504. It can also be seen from U.S. 666. It is not part of a state or national monument, but simply looms large and dreamlike on the horizon, over-whelming the surrounding mesa land.

Chaco Canyon, New Mexico

The Harmonic Convergence, the New Age's first official holiday so to speak, was an unorganized grass-roots day of contemplation and celebration that sprang from nothing to global consciousness in a few short weeks. Based on an ancient Mayan calendar, it was the day that marked our entry into a cataclysmic new era wherein our very evolve-ment and enlightenment would be tested. It was also a celebration of life and the recognition of each individual's responsibility toward healing our planet.

There were gatherings all over the planet at all the power spots: the pyramids; Tor in Glastonbury, England; Tibet; and others. Nevertheless, much publicity and focus fell on one particular ancient site in New Mexico. It was where Jose Arguelles, author of the *Mayan Factor* and progenitor of the Harmonic Convergence, would spend his day of cele-bration.

It was hot and dusty on August 16 in this remote area of northwestern New Mexico. With the dawn the dulcet sounds of folk instruments blended with the breeze and stretched across time to copper bells that had chimed there centuries earlier. It was very beautiful, and the place was Chaco Canyon.

Chaco Canyon is not a pueblo cliff dwelling, nor is it a village ruin. It is the remains of a great Anasazi city complex that includes a large ceremonial and agricultural center with seventy-five surrounding settlements. The Anasazi carefully constructed three hundred miles of wide roads to interconnect these satellite villages. There are easily several hundred ruins and petroglyphs all over the canyon. Even scientists hardly given to hyperbole refer to Chaco Canyon as the Chaco Phenomenon. Here the Anasazi reached their own height and heights we have yet to reach.

In subtle style and achievement, the Chaco culture surpassed that of both the Kayenta and Mesa Verde Anasazi. The people of Chaco Canyon used several different masonry styles, built buildings five stories in height, and utilized passive solar heating. Their architecture was both graceful and functional. It is also undeniably futuristic. Looking at any painting of what Pueblo Bonito in Chaco probably was like in its heyday is like looking at a speculative twenty-second-century space station. Vastly different from medieval castles and the ruins of other cultures, the influence of the pueblo style on southwestern architecture can still be seen.

The Anasazi were benevolent and peaceful people and did not let the hardness of their lives encroach upon their humanity. There is some indication of an elite or decision-making class in Chaco, but nothing of the ilk of the Aztecs or the Mississippian Buzzard Cult. Nor is there evidence that they practiced any form of torture or ceremonial human sacrifice, though they were influenced in other ways by the Mesoamerican cultures from the South. They did, for example, worship the plumed serpent as did both the Mayans and the Aztecs. It is a sacred image that appears repeatedly in Chaco art and petroglyphs.

However, there is evidence that they gathered and redistributed goods according to need. No one went hungry as long as there was food in the city's storage bins. Their trade routes bustled. They imported turquoise, gems, seashells, and the brightly colored feathers of parrots and macaws to fashion them into timeless mosaics and jewelry, which they traded again. Much of their pottery and artworks look as though they could have been designed by today's greatest artists.

They had a complex system of astronomy heavily tied

into their agriculture and religion. They also used bonfires as a communication system between pueblos, forerunning the Native American smoke signal system.

Above all, within Chaco culture was the region's center for worship, feast, and festival. Huge kivas were built for this purpose, primarily in the main center and in all the surrounding settlements. Pueblo Bonito, the largest ruin in Chaco, features thirty-two kivas alone. Tied together by their religion and understanding of the elements, the Chaco Anasazi accomplished what would be impossible today without the use of technology. Phenomenon could be an understatement.

The land of Chaco Canyon is typical of the Four Corners country, high and dry. Evidently it wasn't much different eight centuries ago, except perhaps for a few more inches of precipitation per year. Per the dictates of nature, the extra rain and the lack of it several hundred years later may have been the key to the rise and fall of the Anasazi. Even at that, the abandonment of Chaco appears to have been without strife, if not without grief. The people knew it was time to leave, and clan by clan they drifted away.

Today Chaco Canyon is fairly isolated, sixty miles from the nearest town. You have to drive twenty miles of dirt road, including a steep grade, to get there. Rain makes it impassable.

The ruins blend so completely with the land that you cannot make them out until you are quite close. When they do appear, they are like an optical illusion that comes into focus. As this modern dirt road traverses the ancient highways, the hours spent getting to Chaco Canyon are hours that cut across hundreds of years. Little else matters save sundown.

The sense of timelessness is often called a fourth-dimension experience. It is when our perception of time as it is so rigidly ingrained suddenly changes or becomes distorted. It is the sensation of time standing still, slowing down, or of past and present merging, when all rests in a single moment and the concept of "future time" ceases to exist.

Timelessness is often a part of experiencing Chaco Canyon. At Chaco you are not leaning over a cliffside to get a better look. Here you are surrounded for miles by Anasazi-land, stepping into their perfectly circular kivas, treading their pathways, walking through their doorways, seeing the sky and breathing the air as they did. On the breeze at Chaco you can soon hear bells and instruments, the cries of children, the grinding of corn, and the chatter of folk at work. With the sundown comes the low chant of the Anasazi at prayer as fires are lit in the kivas. Past and present merge. Their spirits still pervade Chaco Canyon.

A few days could easily be spent exploring Chaco. As it is, some people spend decades studying it. Whatever the time spent there, here are a few of the Canyon's spectacular highlights:

Fajada Butte.

This arresting butte can be seen off Route 57 a few miles from the visitor center as you drive into the park. Rising 450 feet above the canyon floor, its summit offers a tremendous view of Chaco. But it is more than that, having been a sun-watching station and quite possibly a sacred mountain for the Anasazi. As with many sun temples for ancient peoples, they used a form of shadow play in which the sunlight at certain times of the year would mark designated stone carvings and rock fissures. Meticulously designed, these shadow plays allowed the astronomer-priests to predict the solar calendar and plant crops. On Fajada Butte, there are petroglyphs and the remains of several rooms where the priests tended to their lonely duties. Archaeoastronomer Ray Williamson talks about the discovery of this use of Fajada Butte in his book, *Living the Sky—The Cosmos of the American Indian*:

> As part of a team making a major rock art survey of the canyon, artist Anna Sofaer was recording the rock art at the top of the butte. While investigating a large peaked spiral hidden behind three large stone slabs on the southeast side of the butte, she was astonished to see a narrow dagger of

Justine Hill

Chaco Canyon—Fajada Butte

light appear on the spiral and begin to move downward across it just to the right of center. In about twenty minutes the spectacular daggerlike appearance was over and the lightning around the spiral had returned to its normal dimness. The fact that she had been there to witness this remarkable event an hour before noon a few days after the summer solstice was a stroke of good luck.

Una Vida.

A short trail leads to Una Vida from the parking lot. Una Vida has a hundred rooms and eight kivas. Though much of Chaco Canyon has been excavated or looted, Una Vida is still only partially excavated, with secrets yet to tell.

Pueblo Bonito.

As Monks Mound is the best-known feature at Cahokia (see Chapter 4), so is Pueblo Bonito for Chaco Canyon. Built in stages beginning about A.D. 900 and occupied for over

Justine Hill

Chaco Canyon—Pueblo Bonito

three hundred years, this pueblo contains eight hundred rooms and thirty-seven kivas. A famed feature of Pueblo Bonito is its remarkable doorways, precisely and beautifully aligned. The Chacoans were serious in their work. Every stone was placed with integrity and care. Pueblo Bonito also features three great kivas. Built without the use of compasses, one of them is perfectly aligned with north-south. It appears that the whole pueblo was built with consideration of the heavens and to capitalize on solar power. It is something we have yet to do today for our complexes. Shaped like the letter D, with its curved wall facing south, Pueblo Bonito's architecture soaked up the sun's rays and kept its residents warm and comfortable throughout the cool nights of fall and winter. During the hot summer, its relationship to the surrounding canyon cliffs offers some shade and cool respite over the main plaza. Pueblo Bonito is brilliant.

Chetro Ketl. Not far from Pueblo Bonito is a pueblo dating back to the 800s. Also very large, Chetro Ketl has five hundred rooms and sixteen kivas. Its central plaza is considered a prime example of Anasazi "classic" architecture. An interesting feature of Chetro Ketl is the tower kiva, built in a cylindrical shape with very high walls. Because Chetro Ketl and Pueblo Bonito are so centrally located at the crossroads of Chaco, it is believed that they were the power centers. The people who lived in these villages made the decisions for all the people of the canyon. If there was an Anasazi elite, they would have resided in Pueblo Bonito or Chetro Ketl.

Casa Riconada.

Truly dramatic, Casa Riconada lies across the canyon from Pueblo Bonito. It was built for one purpose only: worship. Casa Riconada is not a village and has no apartments like the other pueblos. It is a large ceremonial kiva, perfectly circular, almost sixty-six feet in diameter and about fourteen feet deep. It is one of the largest kivas in the Southwest. Exquisite thought and planning were put into its construction, and its full intent is still only theory. Shadow play is also a part of the kiva as beams of light dance through the eastern window on the morning of the summer solstice. The winter solstice also sparks shadow play there. Two T-shaped doorways, aligned with north and south, face each other in the kiva. The four cardinal directions, so sacred to Native Americans, are represented in the very architecture of Casa Riconada. If Casa Riconada was not used as a sky-watching station, then at minimum the Anasazi paid tribute to the sacred elements of their world in how they built the kiva. It is possible that Casa Riconada was not simply used as a place for public gatherings, but may have been a special place of initiation or training for an elite priesthood, the building itself serving as a symbol of the universe. Whatever its full purpose, Casa Riconada stands apart, not only from the other villages, but in its perfect geometry and beauty.

The sites above are only a few of the ruined villages that comprise the Chaco Phenomenon. There are many more.

As you tread the trails to visit these sites and others at Chaco Canyon, take time to find a few of the ancient roads the Anasazi built to connect the settlements. They are far from being anything like primitive trails. Sometimes as wide as thirty feet, the roads have edges that were often marked by wooden beams or rocks. They were built the same as Britain's mysterious ley lines, perfectly straight tracks constructed without notice to the terrain they crossed. Even over steep land, the roads remain straight, with ramps and stairs sometimes cut right into stone. These straight tracks appear all over the world, aligned with the metaphysical power of the planet.

Not to be missed in Chaco Canyon are the many rock paintings. Some of the rock art is in the villages, though much of it is on outlying cliff shelters. The Anasazi weren't the only ones in Chaco Canyon. People go back a long way there, maybe even ten thousand years. Ask for the trail to Atlatl Cave, where rock paintings and arrowheads are evidence of occupation four thousand years ago. On many of the petroglyphs are painted handprints. These handprints are believed to mark the painting as a sacred image or some kind of bridge to the supernatural. The petroglyphs feature religious imagery found throughout the Anasazi world. Besides humans, there are animals, lizards and serpents, fertility themes showing women giving birth, strange creatures we still can't identify, and many flute players. The flute player was very important, connected with life-giving fertility for all things—plants, animals, and humans. The paintings also feature many spirals, an eternal metaphysical image that appears time and again across the world. One stirring rock painting features a star symbol and crescent with a handprint over it. It could possibly represent the sighting of the Crab Nebula supernova in A.D. 1054.

Many Navajo drifted into Chaco Canyon and lived there on and off from the early eighteenth century until the present. They added many of their own artworks to the rock and cliffs of the canyon. Painted Navajo star ceilings and other motifs also appear throughout Chaco.

Chaco Canyon National Historical Park is on Route 57,

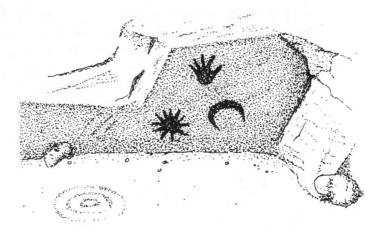

Chaco petroglyphs that could symbolize the A.D. 1054 Crab Nebula supernova. The handprint marks the site as sacred.

which crosses the park north-south. There is a campground at Chaco 1 mile from the visitor center. Gasoline and food all have to be purchased outside of the park in the nearest town or at one of the Navajo trading posts about 27 miles away. The park covers 35,000 acres. Tours and evening lectures are available in the summer and there are 16 miles of trails. For more information, write to or call Superintendent, Chaco Culture National Historic Park, Star Route 4, Box 6500, Bloomfield, NM 87413; (505) 988-6716 or (505) 988-6727.

El Santuario de Chimayo, New Mexico

El Santuario de Chimayo is a very special sacred site in America in that it combines a sensitivity and feeling for Earth religion with Catholicism. Most often throughout the Western Hemisphere, local religion has gone underground as it becomes superseded in society by the more contemporary European religions. Particularly in Central and South America, many people deftly worship both ways, the old and the new, but often at different times of the week. But El Santuario de Chimayo embodies both.

El Santuario de Chimayo is most comparable to the

sacred healing waters of Lourdes in France and is some-times referred to as the American Lourdes. The healing power here, however, comes straight from the Earth. Built in 1816, it is a Catholic chapel built over land reputed to have magical healing powers. Originally it was a healing power source for the Indians. Later, after they had lost the land, its healing powers did not go unrecognized but were resurrected in a new context.

According to the legend, a farmer who was working the land had a holy vision. The visiting angel told him that the land he was plowing was blessed with the martyrdom of two priests who were killed there. Beholden to their death, the land now had healing powers. As the farmer dug beneath the land, he found a cross and a piece of cloth belonging to the martyred priests. To this day, the cross is in the chapel the farmer built. Since then, hundreds of seekers of all backgrounds have visited the chapel to take some of the sacred soil with them. No matter how much of it is taken, the earthen well always fills up again. The chapel is filled with crutches and wheelchairs cast off by those miracu-lously healed.

The chapel and surrounding setting are both picturesque and serene. The atmosphere is solemn and introspective. This chapel and other nearby places of worship are filled with handcrafted altars and personal offerings to such patron saints of New Mexico as Our Lady of Guadalupe and Saint Francis of Assisi. The offerings include photographs, flowers, rosaries, jewelry, letters, poems, and devotional prayers as testimony to the healings visitors have experi-enced. Even for the most cynical visitor, the feeling that permeates El Santuario de Chimayo can be affecting. It is clear that many people have come to this place grieving and left it renewed.

El Santuario de Chimayo is at the eastern end of the small town of Chimayo. It is 10 miles east of Espanola, New Mexico, on the Truchas Road (Route 76), a beautiful scenic road that runs between Santa Fe and Taos. For more infor-mation, write to or call El Santuario de Chimayo, P.O. Box 235, Chimayo, NM 87522; (505) 351-4889.

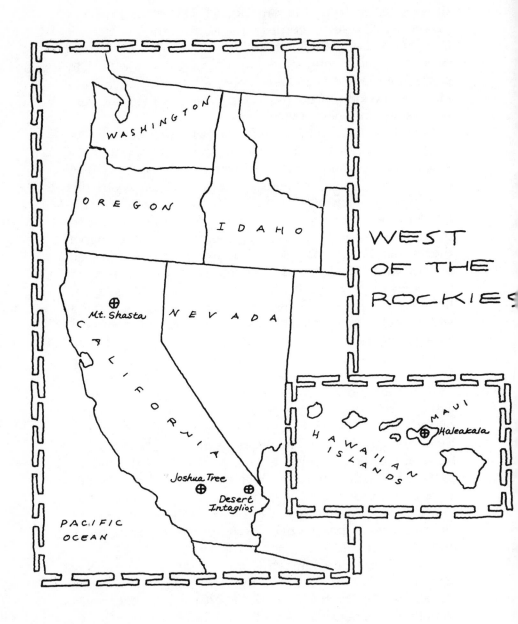

WASHINGTON

OREGON

IDAHO

WEST
OF THE
ROCKIES

⊕
Mt. Shasta

NEVADA

CALIFORNIA

MAUI
⊕ Haleakala

HAWAIIAN ISLANDS

Joshua Tree
⊕

⊕
Desert
Intaglios

PACIFIC
OCEAN

8
WEST OF THE ROCKIES: ALL LANDS STRANGE AND WONDERFUL

People who do not live in California associate the huge West Coast state with things both weird and wonderful. Some of the most common buzzwords are *earthquakes*, *beaches*, *Hollywood*, and *lunatics*.

Californians associate their home with beaches, for sure, and a host of many other gifts, including sun, skiing, redwood forests, wine country, desert hot springs, and mountains. Weekends in California often mean hitting the road for the great outdoors, and few people do it more often than California's urbanites. The state lends itself to retreating from the travails of day-to-day stress. Desert valleys, mountain ranges, and pine forests all neighbor one another. A body can escape from a hot, smoggy day in Los Angeles to an alpine village in a few short hours. Distance and destination take on a new meaning as driving four or five hours for a weekend's jaunt in the wilderness is nothing, most often considered quite worth it. Or, fly four or five hours to Hawaii.

Getting away is important in this land west of the Rockies, as are retreats to renew body and spirit. Especially spirit. For many Californians, the Bill of Rights includes life, liberty, and the pursuit of enlightenment. Entire towns such as Ojai and Mt. Shasta (at the base of the mountain) are considered spiritual centers where many different groups converge for esoteric study, meditation, and practice. It is all over the place; spiritually oriented ashrams, camps, health resorts, sweat lodges, even conventions present a metaphysical alphabet of everything from alchemy to Zen.

Cynics take heed. Until you have listened to the spirits of the redwoods, watched the sunset from Big Sur, or spent the night on Mt. Shasta, watch your words. Once you have tried it, you may sheepishly be singing a different tune.

Joshua Tree National Monument, California

Joshua Tree National Monument has an aura about it that extends far beyond its borders. Tucked away in southcentral California's desert basin, it beckons as a place of peace and solitude. People go there primarily to cool out from burn-out, but this can sometimes be a pretention. Joshua Tree is a place not only of surreal beauty but of supernatural experience. This is its true, but often unmentioned, reputation. For those who open the doors, Joshua Tree's serenity gives way to heightened, sparkling sensations that both tease and caress. Some people love it and use this stimulation for creating. Joshua Tree is known as a great place to write. Others cannot stand it and find themselves restless and uneasy here, anxious to get away.

For several decades, it has been a favorite refuge for the rock 'n' roll community. Many of rock's brightest stars have found a soul place in Joshua Tree's healing warmth, arriving exhausted and leaving inspired with a new vision and a new song. It is their work that has made Joshua Tree part of international consciousness.

Most of the park is Mojave Desert, which is higher in altitude, cooler, and less dry than its lower desert counterpart. This is the home of the inimitable Joshua tree, which is, in fact, a tree.

Dick Arentz, Courtesy of Etherton Gallery, Tucson, Arizona

Joshua Tree—Cholla

The first settlers to the area called these unique trees "ugly and scraggly." Later Mormon settlers had a much more sublime vision. They saw the trees, with their branches raised to the heavens, as symbolic of Joshua's prayers. Thus they were named.

Native Americans had their own version, acutely attuned to how the desert comes alive at night. Many desert creatures avoid daylight's hot sun and wait for darkness to come out of their shelters. The owls leave their burrows, and the coyotes start singing. The stars shimmer with intensity in the clear, dry air of the desert as the bobcat moves through the shadows following a rabbit or desert rat. The yucca night lizard awakens, and the spirits of the Joshua trees begin to dance in the moonlight. When dawn breaks, their furious dance ends, and they are once again frozen, arms raised within the trees, where they await night's frenzied rhythms to start dancing again. Perhaps it is these spirits the rockers tune into, or turn into, at Joshua Tree.

Joshua Tree's half million acres are part of three desert

systems, each with its own unique geology, vegetation, and
wildlife. Along with the Mojave Desert area, the eastern part
of the park is low-altitude Colorado Desert and features the
strange jumping cholla cactus. The jumping cactus is low
to the ground and has sharp long needles. You don't need
to brush against it to get pricked. It is so attracted to water
that should you simply get close enough, say a few inches
to a foot, it will literally jump from its place and embed itself
in your flesh for a refreshing drink. It is all part of Joshua
Tree's dual nature. What is initially so innocuous and peace-
ful-looking has a hidden side patiently waiting for the opportunity to spring to life.

The third desert system in Joshua Tree is the oasis. Here
there are five of them in a lush departure from the surrounding terrain. Looking over a real desert oasis conjures
so many images of settlers and wagon trains. You can

Joshua trees. Legend has it their spirits dance at night.

practically see them, parched to the core, blessing the life-giving water after enduring days across desert lands. Miners stayed at Joshua Tree looking for gold. Mostly they failed, except for the Lost Horse Mine, which did for a time yield some gold, silver, copper, and crystal. Their three now-abandoned mines are still at the park.

People have lived in Joshua Tree as far back as 3000 B.C. These first inhabitants, the Pinto Basin people, left arrowheads, tools, and rock art behind them. Later tribes added to Joshua Tree's numerous petroglyphs, which are hidden away from general view.

Large groups of rocks formed from monzonite quartz dot the land at Joshua Tree and greatly add to its surreal quality. Some of these natural rock sculptures have names, including Jumbo Rocks, Skull, and Trojan. Frequent visitors to Joshua Tree often find or gravitate to their own favorite rock sculpture, where they return again and again. That's a good idea, because it is very easy to get lost in Joshua Tree. Though each rock and tree is unique, the mind wanders here on a hike, and one view to the next becomes labyrinthine in quality. For many reasons, the park rangers will warn you to stay on established roads and trails. This is one of them.

Joshua Tree National Monument is 140 miles east of Los Angeles. Take Route 62 north off Interstate 10 to the town of Joshua Tree and follow the signs into the park. If you continue on Route 62 past Joshua Tree, it will lead you to the town of Twentynine Palms and the Oasis Visitor Center. These are on the north side of the park. Another visitor center, the Cottonwood, is on the south side of the park off Interstate 10 just east of Route 195. There are nine campgrounds and other accommodations in the nearby towns. The park is open year round. For more information, write to or call Superintendent, Joshua Tree National Monument, 74485 National Monument Dr., Twentynine Palms, CA 92277; (619) 367-7511.

The Desert Intaglios, California

Sometime during the last five hundred years a group of Native Americans created a tribute to their gods. Deep in the dry desert, where temperatures soar near the California-Arizona border, they created two large figures in the ground by scraping away the blackish desert gravel to uncover the light earth underneath. Because this desert area has changed little over the centuries, the figures have survived.

The largest figure is a ninety-four-foot-tall man with outstretched arms. Nearby is the carving of a four-legged animal. At the animal's feet is the symbol of the spiral.

There are only theories as to which people carved the figures. Oddly enough, none of the local tribes claim them or the area they are on as sacred. They would have to have been the work of a nomadic tribe, perhaps one that was working its way to the coast after the Spanish invasion of the Southwest.

The Pima Indians of Arizona are descendants of the Hohokam. It is possible that they or several of their clans fled here to escape persecution. This small area in the middle of nowhere became ritual ground. A partial circle that cuts across the man could be the mark of a ritual dance. If the male figure represents one of their gods, the animal remains a mystery. It could be a deer, horse, or mountain lion. Were it a horse, the intaglio definitely would have been created after the arrival of the Spanish, who brought and introduced horses to the Southwest.

Other intaglios featuring creatures, stick men, and serpents can be found in the region. There are two other intaglio sites near Blythe, one in Ripley, another in Winterhaven, and a serpent intaglio near Parker, Arizona. The best bets for getting directions would be to find someone in the archaeology department of a nearby college, any local museums, the local Highway Patrol or Bureau of Land Management. They were all done in very obscure places, and some of them may be on private land. Certainly there are others that have not even been discovered yet.

The intaglios were unknown until air travel, when they were spotted by a pilot in 1931. Like the lines of the Nazca Valley in Peru, the intaglios are visible from the ground, but their clear and full impact becomes evident only when looking down from the sky.

Because the figures are only scraped into the ground, they are fragile in that any intrusion also leaves its mark. As word of the intaglios got around, visitors gathered, and every truck or motorcycle track added to the grounds. Fortunately, in 1963 the figures were saved by the local Boy Scouts, who built a fence around them. Now if they would only build a tower similar to the ones at the Great Serpent Mound and the Rock Eagle Effigy so people could experience their true impact.

The Desert Intaglios are 15 miles north of Blythe, California. From Interstate 10 in Blythe, travel north on Route 95 to the monument marker. The intaglios are under the jurisdiction of the Bureau of Land Management. For more information, write or call the Bureau at 1695 Spruce Street, Riverside, CA 92507; (714) 351-6394.

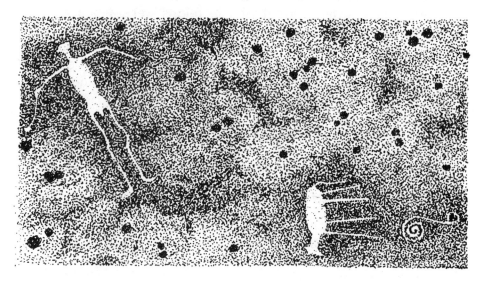

California's desert intaglios.

Mount Shasta, California

The great naturalist John Muir, whose life and unmatched works centered around California's forests and mountains, had this to say when he beheld Mount Shasta in 1886:

> . . . Icy Shasta. . . . When I first caught sight of it over the braided folds of the Sacramento Valley I was fifty miles away, afoot, alone and weary. Yet all my blood turned to wine, and I have not been weary since.

Welcome to Mount Shasta.

Mount Shasta is a sacred mountain to the Indians of northern California, the reputed homeland of the Secret Brotherhood, the place where Lemurian priests hid their magic crystals, a UFO landing spot, a doorway to the fifth and other dimensions, a psychic power source, a great healing mother spirit, a contemporary spiritual center for a vast array of groups, and, in Mystery School teachings, one of nine sacred mountains of the world.

The Indians who once occupied most of the Siskiyou County area where Mount Shasta reigns were a peace-loving people. Though the mountain is named after them, they called it Wyeka, or "Great White." They confirm the very ancient and beloved quality of the mountain in their legend of how it was created, as told by Rosemary Holsinger in *Shasta Indian Tales*:

Great Spirit Makes the Mountain

Great Spirit saw below him that all the land was flat. He thought to make a mountain so high that it could be seen by everyone. He made a hole through the sky. Then he pushed ice and snow down and down, and then he pushed some more down. It made a mound on the flat land below. It grew larger. It grew higher until it became the highest mountain in the land. It was so high that its top pushed its way through the clouds.

Great Spirit stepped down out of the clouds onto his great snowy mountain. Then he stepped down onto the land and looked at his beautiful mountain.

"I will call you Shasta because you are white and pure," he said. "Trees, grow!" he said and many beautiful green pine trees and cedar trees grew fast and tall. "Sun, melt some snow so the trees may drink and remain green!" And Sun did as he was asked, and the water came so fast that rivers and creeks ran full.

"The trees need birds to live in their branches," said Great Spirit as he picked some leaves from the trees. He blew on the leaves and they became birds.

Then Great Spirit felt the birds should have companions. From a tree he took a stick and broke it into many pieces. The small pieces he threw gently into the streams and said, "You are fishes to swim in the streams."

The middle-sized pieces he threw into the forest. "You will become the smaller animals."

The larger pieces he threw about him. "You shall become the largest animal in the forest and shall be called Grizzly Bear." Later, Great Spirit worried about creating Grizzly Bear because that large animal became ferocious.

All became a part of the great mountain.

And that is how it was in the beginning.

Most likely, Shasta is named after a tribe that once lived in the area but is now gone. Some historians dispute this, saying the name is derived from the Russian word *tshastal*, which means "white and pure." It is true that there were many Russian immigrants in the area who filtered down from Alaska. Others insist it comes from the word *chaste*, but final conclusions about the origin of Shasta's name don't exist. The only agreement is that the name is a perfect one.

Shasta itself rises 14,162 feet above sea level and over 10,000 feet above the surrounding terrain. It dominates the landscape for a couple of hundred miles in all directions. Traveling north-south on Interstate 5, it takes several hours to pass it by. Mount Shasta is tremendous.

"As lone as God, and white as a winter moon." That beautiful, well-known description written by Joaquin Miller in 1875 succinctly captures Shasta's holy presence and magnetism. As a teenager he lived in a cabin on Mount Shasta's slopes. When he wrote "Life Among the Modocs" in London in 1873, he introduced Shasta to the world. And it does draw people to it, exactly like a magnet. Once seen, it is not easily forgotten.

Those who visit Shasta often have a very personal relationship with the mountain. Much more than a vacationland or even a soul place, the Shasta lover refers to the mountain not as "it," but as "she." She becomes a friend, a feminine warrior spirit who teaches and sometimes reprimands, but who always nurtures. Whether you're a seeker or otherwise, the Shasta experience is rife with meaning and feeling, its significance one of growth and the feeling usually a blissful one.

The metaphysical mysteries surrounding Mount Shasta are both many and varied.

Shasta is purportedly home to all sorts of spirits and beings, the least of which are human, but that are for the most part humanoid. The most pervasive rumor links Shasta to a secret priesthood of the advanced Lemurians, who fled here when their great continent of Mu (or Lemuria) in the Pacific exploded and sank. Many believe that Shasta is simply a surviving part of Mu, protecting those who gathered on her high ground. It is said that the tall, shaggy-locked Lemurians are so spiritually attuned that they are able to change their physical bodies into etheric matter (spirit stuff) as they wish, that they live underground near the summit of Shasta, and that they maintain a cache of powerful crystals from their homeland.

Another group of beings hidden away in Shasta are the Yaktayvians, who are part of what is called the "Secret Commonwealth." Their people inhabit several secret cities across the planet. Unique to the Yaktayvians is their use of high-pitched magic bells with which they manipulate the four elements: earth, air, water, and fire. Thus they carved their underground tunnels and provide for themselves. The bells also serve to deter unwary humans from getting too close. Some claim they have heard the Yaktayvian bells. The only earthly analogy to this supernatural audio is Tibetan bells. High in the Himalayas, the Tibetans have

Domingo D. Silva

Mount Shasta

devised a way of creating bells whose sound is so pure and affecting that their use can heal illness, change moods, or put the listener in an instant trance state.

The town of Mount Shasta at the mountain's base has been a spiritual center for twenty or more esoteric study groups for most of this century. As a small town of a similar year round population, it is matched only by Ojai, known primarily for Krishnamurti's long residency and foundation. One of these religious groups, the I AM religion, was established on Mount Shasta when its founder, Guy Ballard, encountered the Ascended Master St. Germain, who gave Ballard the tenets of his knowledge and teachings.

Strange saucerlike clouds often gather and sit on Shasta's summit. They lend visual credence to rumors of extraterrestrial use of the mountain. After all, what better place is there for an E.T. dropoff and pickup point, not to mention refueling station for the spaceship?

Native Americans in the region beheld Shasta as a sacred mountain. Many of their morality tales and religious stories take place on Shasta and often feature their most well-loved characters, such as the clever Coyote, the Eagle, and the Great Spirit, as well as beautiful maidens and young warriors. However, as at Shiprock, they discouraged climbing to Shasta's summit, but more for practical reasons than spiritual ones, like the risk of freezing to death.

Mount Shasta is included in the Shasta-Trinity National Forest, which contains 38,200 acres. The town of Mount Shasta, near the base of the mountain, lies in a basin and is bordered by the Klamath Mountains to the west and the Cascade Range of volcanoes to the east, to which Shasta belongs.

Correct. Shasta is a volcano, not a mountain. As part of the Cascade Range, it is in the lively company of about seventeen volcanoes that include Mount Saint Helens, Mount Rainier, and Lassen Peak. Shasta is the largest and may be the most beautiful mountain of the Cascade Range.

For now, Shasta is dormant and definitely not extinct. Could it blow its top again? Possibly, but probably not for another three hundred years. Scientists say that Shasta has erupted every five hundred years for the last twenty thousand years or more. The last eruption was in 1786, so one is not due for a long time. The Mount Saint Helens eruption seems to have had no effect on Shasta, whose eruptions appear to have been much smaller anyway. So don't worry about it or let it stop you from visiting. There would be plenty of warning and ample time to clear out, literally days before an explosion. It is constantly and carefully monitored for heat buildup, trembling, and other signs of volcanic activity.

Furthermore, Shasta is not a single peak, but two peaks or cones. Almost two thousand feet below the Shasta crest is the Shastina cone, with a 12,330-foot elevation. Shasta and Shastina together support five small glaciers. The snow and ice complicate climbing and hiking around Shasta, and safe conduct is imperative. The rangers today do not discourage climbing but strongly warn the climbers, requesting information in case of a rescue operation and recommending the summer months for smoother going. They do warn of avalanches in winter and spring.

Temperatures can be extreme and change suddenly with a storm, cloud cover, or the sunset. The big three hazards of visiting Shasta are hypothermia, altitude sickness, and sunburn. Hypothermia in particular is both terrifying and deadly. It seems to sneak up on people on Shasta, and you would do best knowing how to identify and treat it. Sasquatches, however, are of no concern, there are none. Being hypnotized by a Yaktayvian bell, meeting a star person, or being confronted by a Lemurian are not considered hazards but honors.

Shasta is a favorite summer retreat and a winter wonderland. There are areas provided for alpine and cross-country skiing, snowmobiling, ice fishing, skating, and snow play. There are numerous trails from popular day hikes to isolated wilderness treks. The same goes for backpacking and camping. Some of the campgrounds get very populated during the summer months; others will fulfill your search for solitude. There are a few roads that will take you partially up and around the mountain, including the Old Military Pass Road and the Everett Mountain Highway that takes you to the Shasta Ski Bowl at a 7,703-foot elevation.

To reach **Mount Shasta**, take Interstate 5, which runs north-south through central California. Take the Essential exit to go to the Mount Shasta Ranger Station or the McCloud/Shasta exit to go to the McCloud Ranger Station. If you are within 100 miles of Mount Shasta, you cannot miss it. For more information, write to or call District Ranger, Mount Shasta Ranger District, 204 West Alma, Mount Shasta, CA 96067, (916) 926-4511; or District Ranger, McCloud Ranger District, P.O. Box 1620, McCloud, CA 96057, (916) 964-2184. For information on what is available in the city of Mount Shasta, write to or call the Chamber of Commerce, 300 Pine St., Mount Shasta, CA 96067; (916) 926-4865.

The Doorway to Different Dimensions

Sandy has been involved in metaphysical and spiritual work for her whole life. There are two places on Earth with which she feels a most profound connection: Mount Shasta, California, and Ayers Rock in Australia.

"When I got to Shasta it was the dead of night—almost two in the morning. Even before I got there, starting with Sacramento, I could feel a pulsating energy, and I knew it was the mountain. It is a magnet for me, definitely a power source. So I'm driving and hearing the mountain pulse, hearing its heartbeat, hearing it talk to me. And there, at the same time, was another, slower heartbeat. I felt drawn to it, and I felt a beautiful motherliness, a peaceful, comforting warmth. It was like a big breast for me. I slept at the foot of the mountain and woke up in her shadow. I slept there again on my return trip.

"Shasta is the doorway to another dimension. It is the tingling feeling of the wind on your cheeks even when there is no wind. What I've discovered since that time is that it's an experience of fifth-dimensionality, time and timelessness being the fourth, and the fifth being a most playful, loving sensation beyond time or place. That was the question I asked, and the answer I received was, 'You're in it. Play. Have fun.'

"In August of '87 I was there between the 14th and the 23rd. That feeling of fifth-dimensionality went on all week. Everything got softer; the cars didn't make as much noise, people didn't make as much noise. There was a sweet, hushed harmony among everything. Everyone felt it and contributed. They were there for a holy reason as well. There was a lot of respect.

"Fourth dimension is time, feeling the nowness of past, present, and future all at once. That's what we're all heading for. From there it's easier for us to experience the

fifth dimension. It's the next step to higher awareness and leaving our bodies. In metaphysics, there is the theory that all things happen simultaneously—past-life flashbacks, future flashes, moving spatially, astral projection. It's all part of that. Spirituality requires understanding and developing, not merely going through the form of spirituality, the rituals. It's fulfilling yourself with the content.

"So when I posed my question, 'Show me the fifth dimension,' that's when I realized and got my answer, 'You're in it.' Repeatedly. Finally I got it. They're telling me to jump in the water and have fun and that it's no big deal. It's no different from being in tune anywhere else. But on Shasta, there's a facility. She makes it a whole lot easier to expand.

"It may sound like I didn't have this galvanizing, magical experience. But I wasn't asking for a lot. I wasn't on a vision quest. Even so, look at what I got in return."

Haleakala National Park, Hawaii

All Hawaii is magic land, paradise on Earth. Hawaiians would probably find it a useless task to try to pinpoint any one sacred site in these enchanted islands because they know all Hawaii is sacred. Hawaii is considered more than an energizing power source on the planet's energy matrix. It is considered one of Earth's chakras.

More than a place that embodies secrets of the past, Hawaii is the Land of the Living Gods. Those who doubt or, even worse, laugh at the vitality of Hawaii's reigning spirits rarely get the last laugh. The joke has rested mainly on some of Hawaii's overeager land developers, who in their zeal to pave paradise have learned the hard way. Not heeding the warnings of the wise, they sometimes end up watching their half-million-dollar homes crumble one by one into the sea or get trounced by lava. Pele, Hawaii's dramatic Fire Goddess (as in volcanic activity), sometimes gets very touchy. They all do. Tragedies do happen, even in paradise. Hawaii's living gods can be rather implacable. As the Hawaiians themselves will tell you, should you go there hell bent on breaking taboos and insulting the spirits, make sure your ticket home is on standby. You may not want to hang around.

The native religion of Hawaii is Kahuna, as her gods are Kahuna gods. Kahuna is oriented toward positive living and fulfillment. It is as much a philosophy as it is a religion and accounts for three states of mind, not dissimilar to modern psychology's subconscious, conscious, and superconscious states. With each mind is a life energy that can be used for different purposes.

No matter what their beliefs, few dispute the fact that should you arrive in Hawaii blue and exhausted, a week later you will be a new person.

Aloha.

Haleakala National Park is on the island of Maui, the second largest of Hawaii's 124 islands, whose beauty is legendary. The park is centered around the huge, dormant Haleakala volcano, whose crater is a massive, breathtaking wonder. It is another world from the lush orchid gardens and waterfalls of Hawaii as it is from all the world. Haleakala may be the closest place on Earth to a bona fide moonscape.

Haleakala is the handiwork of the gods. Its name means "House of the Sun," and it is the place where restless souls go to find peace. It is called House of the Sun because this is where Maui, one of Hawaii's gods, captured the Sun. Maui, a rather clever mischief-maker, wanted more daylight to pursue his love of fishing. In the dark hours of the morning, he climbed to the summit of Haleakala, where the Sun would pass by close overhead. As each of the Sun's rays crept over the crater's edge, Maui snared it with his magic ropes and tied it down. He refused to free the Sun until he had agreed to slow his daily trek across the skies. In this way, Maui and the people of the island received more daylight for fishing.

Rising 10,023 feet above sea level, Haleakala is one of the largest craters on the planet. Covering about nineteen square miles, it is as large as Manhattan. Taking the road up to the summit can be dizzying. It is the only road in the world where you go from sea level to 10,000 feet in just forty miles. In that forty miles you will go from tropical beaches to semitropical pasturelands to the lava-rock-strewn slopes of the crater. You will also go from T-shirts to jackets as the temperature drops up to thirty degrees. Higher than the clouds, surrounded by ocean, with the islands far in the distance, it offers a spectacular view and the feeling of truly being part of the sky.

One feature not to be missed at Haleakala is the Leleiwi Overlook. It is six miles above the Haleakala visitor center. With the right conditions of a cloud layer and the late afternoon sun, you can see the Specter of the Brocken. This visual marvel is named after Brocken Mountain in East Germany, which features the same phenomenon. The late afternoon sun will project your ghostlike image on the clouds, surrounded by a colorful rainbow.

Though Maui may have captured the sun in Haleakala, the spirit of the crater belongs to Madame Pele. Three areas

Michael Baskin

Haleakala Crater

of the crater are named after her. Pele's Paint Pot is near the center of the crater and features stone formations of yellow and red. Nearby is Pele's Pig Pen, which looks like a livestock corral. Keanawilinau or Bottomless Pit is an old spatter vent that spewed globs of lava when the volcano was alive. Legend has it that the Bottomless Pit was where Kamakokahai, the Sea Goddess and Pele's sister, tried and failed to enter the volcano to quench its fires.

Being down in Haleakala is once again entering another world from standing on the summit. It is a world of golds, oranges, and grays. Many of the plants and animals in this barren place are few and far between, making their appearance all the more precious. It is home to the beautiful and peculiar silversword, a silver sea anemone type of plant that blooms only once a year. In bloom, its tower of gold, pink, and dark red flowers can rise up six feet. There are a few wild mountain goats, descendants of those introduced a few centuries earlier by missionaries. And here you can listen to the soft, humanlike call of the nene, a black-headed goose that lives only in Hawaii. Mostly, however, you will hear only silence and your own breathing.

Daniel Giamario, who conducts astrologically oriented vision quests in Haleakala, wrote, "It is the only place I know where the inner sounds become greater than the outer sounds."

Devoid of distractions, surrounded by a quiet yet awesome beauty, Haleakala crater may be the quintessential place for inner and spiritual work. It is large enough, isolated enough, and stays relatively unpopulated. Descending into Haleakala and camping down there for more than a day or two won't be for everybody. You have to be quite ready to enjoy moments of nothing but your own heartbeat and your own thoughts. It is very Zen and very basic.

There are two visitor centers, the Haleakala Park Headquarters at 9,745 feet and the Puu Ulaula Visitor's Center near the summit. One mile from the visitor's center is Science City, an astronomical research station. One of its many solar and lunar research projects includes bouncing a beam of laser light off the prisms that were left on the moon by the astronauts.

The only way down into the crater is by hiking or riding horseback on the park's thirty miles of trails. Backpacking and primitive camping in the crater are allowed. There are a few overnight cabins near the crater floor, mostly built to help out unprepared hikers. The park is open year-round.

Something very special to try at Haleakala is offered by the Maui Mountain Cruisers. They will pick you up in the middle of the night, and for the next eight hours you will be driven to the summit of the crater for the sunrise and breakfast. Then you get a mountain cruiser bicycle to glide down 38 miles of countryside with stops along the way to take in the views and historical sites, ending with lunch. They can be reached by writing or calling Maui Mountain Cruisers, PO Box 1356, Makawao, Maui, HI 96768; (808) 572-0195. For more information, write to or call Haleakala National Park, PO Box 369, Makawao, Maui, HI 96768; (808) 572-9306. Should you call Hawaii, keep in mind that its time is three hours earlier than Pacific time on the West Coast.

Daniel and the Goat King

Daniel, a vision quest guide, spends the last five days of every year in Haleakala crater. There he does inner work and plans the year ahead.

"This last time in Haleakala there was a very bad storm, and I took refuge in a goat's cave. There are a lot of wild mountain goats that live in the crater, and I spent five days taking shelter there. It was my base, situated on a great high point in the middle of the crater.

"One of the issues I've always faced in my life is the patriarchy complex. That's the idea that you always have to do better and better, that you're never doing enough, and that the rewards are out there somewhere.

"I happened to have a book with me, an excellent book called The Scapegoat Complex *by Sylvia Pererra, which is about going back to the original Goat God that pre-dated the Yom Kippur ritual in Judaism. They would send the goat out into the wilderness with all the sins of the community on its back. The book is about how that ritual degenerated into a complete separation from our primal, passionate, organic, instinctual ecstasy that goes with being human—that was the Goat God and how those sides of ourselves became the scapegoat.*

"So anyway, here I am in a goat cave reading this book. And the first night I was there a group of mountain goats entered the cave. First there was the King of the Goats, clearly the leader of the pack, and behind him were seven more. They were like his lieutenants. And he confronted me. It was as if he came into the cave and said, 'What the hell are you doing in my cave?' Well, there was nowhere to run or escape. They could have charged me. I was scared, but I had no other choice but to deal with him. I had to make an agreement with him and give him an offering and say, 'When was the last time you saw a human trying to be a goat? I need your cave for a few days. I need shelter.' And then he looked at

me a long time and left, the others following him. They were beautiful, too, with horns and long golden coats. I was a little shaken, but also felt very strong and resilient.

"Near the end of the experience I found a goat's skull. In the book I was reading, an ancient ritual was described where you cleanse yourself by pouring an oil or potion, which symbolically would contain all of your ills and problems, onto a goat's skull. So I ended my quest by doing that ritual. It worked."

SELECTED
BIBLIOGRAPHY

Bakker, Elma, and Richard Lillard. *The Great Southwest.* Palo Alto, CA: American West, 1972.

Bridges, Marilyn. *Markings—Aerial Views of Sacred Landscapes.* New York: Sadev Books, 1986.

Casey, Robert L. *Journey to the High Southwest.* Seattle: Pacific Search West, 1985.

Cazeau, Charles, and Stewart Scott. *Exploring the Unknown—Great Mysteries Reexamined.* New York: Plenum Press, 1979.

Eddy, John A. "Probing the Mystery of the Medicine Wheels," *National Geographic.* January 1977.

Folsom, Frank. *America's Ancient Treasures.* New York: Rand McNally, 1971.

Haining, Peter. *Ancient Mysteries.* New York: Taplinger Publishing Co., 1977.

Hibbin, Frank. *Digging Up America.* New York: Hill and Wang, 1960.

Hoffman, John. *Sedona and Oak Creek Canyon.* Flagstaff, AZ: Canyonlands Publications, 1987.

Holsinger, Rosemary. *Shasta Indian Tales.* Happy Camp, CA: Naturegraph Publishing, 1982.

Kennedy, Ira. "Dreaming the Myth Onward," *The Highlander.* Marble Falls, TX, 1987.

Krupp, E. C. *In Search of Ancient Astronomies.* New York: McGraw-Hill, 1979.

Mack, Jim. *Haleakala—The Story Behind the Scenery.* Las Vegas, NV: KC Publications, 1979.

McGlone, William R. and Phillip M. Leonard. *Ancient Celtic America.* Fresno, CA: Panorama West Books, 1986.

Michell, John. *New View over Atlantis.* New York: Harper and Row, 1983.

Rathbun, Shirley. *First Encounters—Indian Legends of Devil's Tower.* Sand Creek, WY: Sand Creek Printing, 1982.

Sacred Circles. Kansas City, MO: Nelson Gallery of Art— Atkins Museum of Fine Arts, 1977.

Silverberg, Robert. *Mound Builders of Ancient America.* Greenwich, CT: New York Graphics Society, Ltd., 1968.

Snow, Dean. *The Archeology of North America.* New York: Viking Press, 1976.

Stewart, George and Jean Stewart. *The Mysterious Maya.* Washington, D.C.: National Geographic Society, 1977.

Sutphen, Dick. *Sedona: Psychic Energy Vortexes.* Malibu, CA: Valley of the Sun Publishing, 1986.

Terrell, John. *The American Indian Almanac.* New York: Thoms Y. Crowell Co., 1971.

Thomas, D. H. *The Southwestern Indian Detours.* Phoenix, AZ: Hunter Publishing Co., 1978.

Trento, Salvatore Michael. *The Search for Lost America.* Chicago: Contemporary Books, 1978.

Van Cleef, A. *The Hot Springs of Arkansas.* Golden, CO: Outbooks, 1971.

Vaughn, Ralph E. "The Desert Giants of Blythe," *The Unexplained.* Premier Issue, 1987.

Waters, Frank. *Book of the Hopi.* Middlesex, England: Penguin Books, 1983.

Wetherill, Benjamin Alfred. *The Wetherills of Mesa Verde.* Rutherford, N.J.: Farleigh-Dickinson University Press, 1977.

Williamson, Ray A. *Living the Sky—The Cosmos of the American Indian.* Norman, OK: University of Oklahoma Press, 1984.

Index